ROBERT H. BAKER

A Legacy of Small Craft

ROBERT H. BAKER

A Legacy of Small Craft

Anne W. Baker

Sarah H. Baker
PO Box 39
Cape Canaveral, FL 32920

First printing: October 2014

Front cover photograph by Shirley Utterback.

Printed in the United States of America.

Years ago I became obsessed with seventeenth- and eighteenth-century houses, most of which were falling down but still had a story to tell and parts and pieces that could be saved—old and forgotten pieces that held an abundant amount of architectural history. I began to collect whatever I could fit in my 1950 station wagon and in no time my barn was filled with treasures. My family was not impressed—my father only saw as far as the scratches on the new station wagon he'd given me. My sister called it my "silly phase." My then-husband wondered whom he had married, and if my mother had been alive, she would have agreed with them all. BUT not Bob Baker, who was doing the same thing at his barn—except his treasures were old and forgotten New England small craft.

This is Bob's story—his and mine. Some of it took place before I met him and some afterwards.

—AWB

Contents

Foreword

A Legacy of Small Craft is the story of a man's life as seen through the eyes of a woman who loved and admired him. The man is Robert H. Baker (1927–1983), known to most as "Bob"; the woman is Anne W. Baker (1929–2011), known to most as "Pete," but called "Petey" only by her closest friends. I am their youngest child, Sarah, and it falls to me to share this story with you.

This story was meant to be told, but it was a long time forming. Shortly after my father's death in 1983, my mother made her first attempt at a book, but she was not ready to write this story and put the project aside. For years she would tackle some bit of the account, producing several articles about boats and eventually a book about herself, *Collecting Houses*.

Then, in 2010, after years of starting and stopping, she began pulling the layers together and the story came to life. When she died unexpectedly in 2011, the manuscript was mostly finished and with the invaluable help of close family friends, her story of my father can now be told.

On the surface one might categorize my mother as old buildings—houses, mills, barns, etc.—and my father as traditional working craft, the workingman's boat. But like everyone, there were other layers for each. At his core, Dad was a time, an understanding, a way of seeing that is being lost in these days of technology. How he would have handled computers and cell phones, I can't begin to image. My mother embraced technology and used it, at least if it proved useful to her goals, such as writing this book, scanning negatives and pictures, using email, and the Internet.

After my mother's death, I discovered my parents in a totally new way through looking at their papers, the books in their library, the possessions collected over their lifetimes that not only decorated the house, but filled workshops and storage buildings, and in the people whom they called friends.

My mother was a truly amazing individual. I have always been aware that she taught herself everything she knew about anything. She did not go to college or attend trade school. She read books, attended seminars, and went out and did things. She taught herself well and become a recognized authority on old building, the maker of highly sought-after pottery, the creator of extensive gardens, and an accomplished writer, to name just a few of her talents. While I was preparing her personal collections to be archived, I discovered that she kept detailed notes about every project she undertook. While I would not call her an affectionate mother—her manner of teaching was in line with her personal style of learning: get the tools and teach yourself from books or by looking at examples—I learned much from her that has helped, in part, to form the strong woman I have become, unafraid of a challenge.

My father, by contrast, was very affectionate with me as well as with his other children and the children of friends and family. If you wanted to learn something he knew, he was there to teach you. While I learned about "learning" from my mother, I learned about "how" from my father—how to hold and use a tool most effectively without cutting yourself, to use the right tool for the job, to use wood on wood and metal on metal, and techniques of construction. I was seventeen when he passed away, so there was a lot I never had a chance to learn well, but Dad left me with a foundation of skills and memories of his teachings that guide me in everything. I learned some of the most important lessons which I carry today, such as: "If you're going to take time to do it, take time to do it right" or "Always leave it cleaner than you found it—especially when you are working in someone else's space."

I recall times when Dad would be busy working on a boat in his shop but he would always make a space for me to watch, to help (as only a wide-eyed five year old can), to ask a question, or to get guidance on some project. Or there were the times when one of us might mention wanting to go rowing; work would temporarily stop, a small dingy was launched outside the shop, a "recovery line" was securely attached to boat and land, a lifejacket was produced for the rower (and any interested passengers) to don, a helping hand enabled all to get aboard, a few words of instruction were offered, and you were released from the hold of land, off to play in worlds of your imagination, to figure out your frustrations and triumphs, and to be rescued should you just call out.

Through preparing this book for printing I have learned that boats were part of who my father was from a very young age, but I knew him as also loving old cars, old trains, steam engines, old buildings, and photography. I remember him as an outwardly quiet man, but as I think of the "adventures" he took me on, I recall how his deep passions expressed themselves. More than once we entered a "closed" boatyard, tromped through fields or over marshes or mashed weeds out of the way behind someone's barn, all in the quest of the next boat. When not out looking for boats, we'd explore along the edges of Edaville Railroad in Carver, Massachusetts, looking for abandoned train cars, and through old train yards throughout New England. We'd be off climbing on old tractors long forgotten in a field or in the corner of some old barn. On a rainy day, or when there was not any work needing to be done, Dad might pull out a miniature steam engine and get it running again, or maybe he would work on the set-up for his small-gauge trains. When it wasn't boats, trains, or steam engines, it might be cars or photography.

These were my parents. This was my childhood. It was not about nine-to-five hours or "normal" work-a-day activities or typical gender roles. It was about passions, interests, and getting the job done well, correctly, and on time, when possible. It was about respecting the wood, the tools, and the heritage. The Quakers have a saying: Let your life speak. Dad was a quiet, humble man. Let these pages tell his story through the eyes of my mother.

Sarah H. Baker

A Vintage Yacht

Familiar words. "Oh Petey, look at her!" I looked. I saw a derelict boat tied to a wharf. I looked back at Bob. His eyes, the color of polished green glass, glowed as if the tide had just washed over them. It didn't matter that we were in in Providence, Rhode Island, midway across the Point Street Bridge. Bob switched our Volvo into reverse, and I sensed my life was about to change. It was 1962.

By instinct Bob found the wharf and the boat. Parking next to her, it was quickly obvious that she had been sunk and only recently raised from her grave of murky, stagnant water. Her topsides were covered by a thick growth of slimy seaweed and her decks layered in mud.

But as we watched her gracefully floating back and forth on her lines, it became clear to Bob that she was more than a she—she was a lady.

When her lines eased a bit, we jumped onboard. Amidships on her long narrow body was her deckhouse. Behind the deckhouse was an open bridge and behind it a smokestack—a stack so tall that it cast a shadow on the city's horizon. Despite the cartoon of a sailfish painted on the stack, peeling red paint on the decks, silver paint on the teak deckhouse, and mud everywhere, the cabin trunk, hatches, bridge, and stack had all the elements of a vintage yacht.

But entering the deckhouse we encountered more than mud and seaweed: we encountered havoc. Shards of glass from the arched windows were scattered everywhere; the mahogany paneled walls and overhead were smashed; a door, ripped from its hinges, lay on the floor; and sprawled upside-down in the corner like a beaten-up street urchin was a large round table—evidently the culprit that caused some of the damage. Its battered appearance certainly had a delinquent look about it. At least the two built-in settees, the Shipmate stove, and the German silver sink and countertop in the abutting galley had escaped its terror.

From the galley a companionway led below. Bob grabbed my hand, and as we descended we were enveloped by a suffocating odor of oil, mud, and decay. Dark and full of shadows, the only light was from two portholes, just enough to see that the bilge was a foot deep in oily water and the passage choked with slimy curtains of hanging seaweed. However, I wasn't about to be left behind—Bob was onto something. Offering a nervous nod, I gingerly stepped into the water, sloshed through the bilge, and parted the seaweed like parting beaded curtains in a Third Avenue bistro. We explored the staterooms, crew's quarters, and engine room. The green scum, oil, and seaweed followed. I was used to cobwebs and dirt in old cellars, not scum, oil, and dead seaweed, but Bob was elated. His scrutinizing eyes calmly appraised the workmanship and details, while romanticizing on its past glory with, I was sure, himself as captain.

"Let's buy it," he said.

Sensing my shocked look he explained, "But she's all here, all the original parts and pieces, and they are superb."

In Bob's mind everything had potential and the worst condition awakened his greatest calling. I thought sweat, toil, and labor—and forget our plan to go to California—but his enthusiasm was irresistible. "Why not?" I replied, owning it was a given.

Close by was a bar. Somebody inside might be able tell us about the boat. As we passed through the door, the morning light vanished and the smell of stale alcohol and cigar smoke puckered my nose and made me feel dizzy. Sitting in a booth playing solitaire was a putty-faced man. His weather-lined face, scruffy beard, grease-stained hands, and oil-spattered coveralls suggested he worked on the waterfront and might know something about the boat tied up next to the bar. He shuffled the deck of cards, laid out a new game, then pointed a knobby finger said, "The owner is over there."

A beefy man in a plaid lumber jacket was sitting at the bar nursing a beer. As we approached, his weatherworn face cracked into a smile. He rose, offering a calloused hand.

"Welcome aboard. Tiger's the name," he said. "And yes, the boat

is for sale." Damn if he hadn't been expecting us. That was why I'd had a creepy feeling we were being watched ever since we'd gotten out of our car.

Tiger told us he was a marine salvager and explained that the boat had sunk at her berth in East Greenwich, Rhode Island. Her scuppers, located below the waterline, had plugged with rainwater, then froze and burst.

"She filled with sea water," he said, "sank to the bottom, and the owner wasn't interested in paying to have her raised. Six months later I raised her and towed her to Providence."

His intent, he explained, was to haul her on shore, burn her, then rake the ashes. "Best way to salvage the copper and bronze fittings," he said. He took another swig on his beer and smiled." If you want her she's yours, $2,000 cash."

The day wasn't half over, and we had become the new owners of *Kalmia*.

Named after the botanical word for mountain laurel, *Kalmia* was designed by Cox & Stevens and built by George F. Lawley and Son in 1909. She measured 83 feet with a 14-foot beam and drew only 4 feet

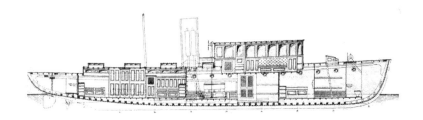

Kalmia Interior Cross Section
1909 *Yachting* magazine

of water. Bob's survey proved her well built. The hull was double planked with yellow pine, double framed with oak, and her keel an 8 x 10-inch piece of white oak. "Excellent construction," Bob said. "That's why she's still around."

The exterior of the deckhouse, hatches, and cabin trunk were paneled in teak. The deck was yellow pine and the interior paneling was Santo Domingo mahogany.

When *Kalmia* was built she was among the first gasoline-powered motor vessels. A few months later we would find an article written in the September 1909 issue of *Yachting* magazine stating that she originally had two Hall-Scott 60-horsepower, 4-cylinder, 4-cycle gasoline engines with a cruising speed of thirteen miles per hour. The article described her as a pretty concrete example of the progress made during the past few years in design and construction of cruising craft propelled by the internal combustion engine. The 1909 article went on to say, "In crafts of the modern type, however, such as this 83-footer, there is to be found not only plenty of stateroom accommodations but a really practical arrangement for the storing of sufficient supplies to allow a long cruise."

Our first cruise, however—Providence to Newport—would not be long. Her engine room was in no condition to even think about power. We pumped her out, threw her bow line to a towboat, and held our breath as *Kalmia* was gently pulled away from the dock.

Underway, I'm sure *Kalmia* was pondering her latest fate, while Bob, the proud captain, leaned back in a beach chair, his feet up on the rail, a beer in hand—ready to salute passersby. I was perched in the bow, and as we made slow headway down Narragansett Bay, I watched her stem cut a silver path through the water, my imagination soaring on the wings of adventure.

Five hours later we reached Norton's Shipyard in Newport, where Frank Norton, owner and friend, had offered a free berth. Frank's boatyard, next to Long Wharf, was situated at the farthest northeast corner of the harbor. You couldn't go any farther. The boatyard was surrounded by interesting old warehouses, but they looked in as bad shape as *Kalmia*. Mostly fishing boats were tied up at Frank's boatyard, and I wondered if he had offered us a free berth thinking he and his fisherman friends might be entertained by two lunatics attempting to restore a derelict yacht.

Frank was a salty waterfront person, corded arms, bull neck, big blunt hands, and in his mind *Kalmia* was just another capitalist's toy. He couldn't understand what we saw in her, but as we scraped off layers of underwater growth and paint applied to the decks by the bucket-and-mop method, Frank become mesmerized by the charm of her era and of her restoration.

Photographs: By Tiger and from personal collection.

Restoration

The word restoration goes back many generations. It's a word that should mean preserving our heritage, but too often restoration implies a complete overhaul, ripping out everything old and replacing with new, a total destruction of the life of the whole.

"Until you come face to face with a boat's structure, you have little comprehension of how to conserve it. A knowledge," Bob commented, "that doesn't come from reading blueprints." Instead of restoration, Bob often used the word conservation. For Bob, conservation meant finding and preserving the spirit given by the hand, eye, and need of the builder: the mysterious suggestions of what had been, and what it had been lost, the gentle parts that the sun and rain had wrought.

Bob believed that those who want to understand and reclaim an old boat must first get familiar with every part of it: its heritage, condition, wear marks, how the pieces were cut, type of wood and fastenings used, and what the original builder had in mind when he built the boat.

"When a piece is beyond repair," Bob said, "it should be copied and built the way it was originally—same shape, type of wood, and fastenings. By the time one is finished replacing rotted pieces, he will have a pretty fair idea of how each piece goes together to make the whole. However, when the boat is beyond repair, its remains must be measured, drawn, and photographed. Without proper documentation, how will anybody know, a hundred years from now, about the secrets of its heritage, the type of tools, paint, lumber, fastenings, etc., that were originally used?"

And when it comes to paint, even though Bob disliked scraping down layer by layer to find the original paint colors, he knew it was part of the conservation process, a process that sometimes required removing a recently installed piece, such as a thwart, to see what color might be behind where the newer piece had been attached. Identifying the original colors, and when possible, their ingredients, was particularly important when boats were to be used to educate, such as a boat on display in a museum.

Bob had strong feelings about good and bad paint. He felt that today's boat paint is formulated to make everything look like fiberglass and devil take the wood. "House paint seems to be the inexpensive answer," he explained. "It's still full of oil, and even without the lead it can be dried in less than a week," he explained. "Oil is the answer—synthetic surface coatings just won't work. Modern marine paint seems to me to be too hard for old wooden boats."

Bob used house paint mixed to order for a particular color, but the color, he felt, was being tinkered with and he didn't really trust it. "The original paint [primer] used on boats must have been good," he said. "It's stayed on in many places for a hundred years. I have found a good deal of original white lead priming in out-of-the way places on many boats. Maybe it's time we started thinking about making our own paint. Admittedly, lead is not available except in small lots under the counter. Time was, you bought a pot of paint for a specific work on boats. Now you buy a pot of all-purpose and hope to hell it sticks on a particular job."

Bob took great pleasure in this work. He loved anything beautiful and good, in particular working with wood, shaping objects, and repairing anything that he liked the looks of. It is not surprising that Bob was interested in such things as restoring a boat; a house; a badly scorched wall of paneling; an omnibus; dismantling, moving, and re-erecting old buildings; carving weathervanes; building boat models; and restoring a vintage yacht.

How Did This Happen?

When Robert Howe Baker was born in November 1927 he had a lot to live up to. His grandfather, Louis McHenry Howe, was President Franklin Roosevelt's private secretary; his grandmother, Grace Howe, was appointed as the first postmistress in the United States; his father, Robert Horace Baker, was a well-known author and teacher of astronomy; his mother, Mary Howe Baker, was a teacher of mathematics; and his godfather was President Franklin Roosevelt.

Instead Robert Howe Baker's arrival was at exactly the right time in the twentieth century to put his own and very opposite talents and natural abilities to their greatest use—his love for boats.

Bobby, as he was called as a child, spent his summers by the ocean in Westport, Massachusetts, a seaside community of fisherman and farmers located next to Fall River, where his mother had grown up.

One summer day in 1935, when Bobby was five, his mother snapped this picture. Natural enough—a cute little boy playing with a toy boat in

the sand dune—but little did his mother realize that she had photographed Bob's future.

By the time he reached his teens he had already been dragging home derelict boats found on the beach. There were skiffs and sharpies and a yard full of orphans to rebuild and experiment with on the river; when he needed a sail, there were always his mother's bed sheets. "Will he ever grow up?" she worried. Out of patience with her son, she announced it was time for tennis lessons.

The boats were childhood fun, but the experiences were nurturing Bob's natural skill and his understanding of watercraft. As he grew older and the yard behind his mother's summerhouse filled with wrecks from the marsh and there were fewer sheets for the beds, his mother could not understand what was happening to her son. Boats did not fit her plans for his future. "Your grandfather," she reminded him, "was Louis McHenry Howe, Franklin Roosevelt's private secretary and instrumental in convincing Roosevelt to run for president."

Despite her disapproval there was no way Bob could resist the exciting possibilities and boat treasures the rivers had to offer. There was *Arrow*, a smack; *Hurricane*, a sharpie; *Teal*, a Swampscott dory; *Typhoon*, a dinghy; *Shipwreck*, a punt; *Green Hornet*, a sharpie; and others.

Bobby was twelve when he found a like-minded friend, ten-year-old Alden Ring. Alden remembers him expertly paddling a 6-foot punt before the southwest wind as he came in with the tide, then rounded to, slipping between the wharves into the calm water of the mooring.

Years later Alden wrote about their experiences.

He was wearing an old-style English submariner hat with dungarees and a loose shirt—tall and well built for age twelve and as skinny as a broomstick. I watched as he pulled that punt up onto the wharf, and as if it were a handbag, he emptied out the water. There was nothing shy about either of us. We immediately started talking about boats, and before long we were on our way to look at my father's old sharpie on the marsh at Westport Point. I showed him the standing gaff rig I'd found after the '38 hurricane, and he surmised, might have been a fisherman's dory rig gone

Arrow

adrift. Later Bob and I had lunch together at his house. I was particularly impressed with the sailing plank-on-frame and rib models he had made. I had made some crude hollowed-out jobs and some scale kit models, but these of Bob's were original, complete and beautifully wrought. That afternoon it rained and we studied old Rudder *and* Yachting *magazines. By the end of the day we had become buddies.*

By the summer of 1944 Bob had somehow acquired an 18-foot, round-bottomed smack boat that he named Arrow. *Rigged as a catboat, she was lapstrake, not very wide, but fast and handy although she leaked a good deal.* Arrow's *mast was heavy, and she often capsized at her mooring. Bob moved her mast aft behind the first thwart and rigged her as a sloop, then later as a ketch. He also built a deck level with the thwarts that stiffened her up some and made her less inclined to leak.*

One bright and clear early spring day, Bob and I decided to sail Arrow *to Cuttyhunk. Because of a strong northeast wind and heavy white-capped seas to contend with, we were close-hauled on the port tack with two reefs while bailing out seawater like crazy.*

After running into the harbor we beached Arrow *next to the wharf then walked up the hill to Ma Allen's, the old hotel on the island. It was Sunday noon. Baked bean sandwiches were all there was to be served. Warm and dry with a great view of Buzzard's Bay, we listened to an old radio playing a remarkable clear performance of the C major Mozart Violin Sonata. We left that afternoon, launched* Arrow, *and were happily tacking along the beach when we were forced to heave-to by the U.S. Coast Guard, who told us that two young boys shouldn't be sailing around out there. We explained we'd sailed across that morning, and I guess they figured we were beyond saving so they let us go. That night it was the bus back to Boston and school for us—an anticlimax, all right.*

During a summer in the early 1940s we took a cruise in Teal *to Noman's Land Island. With* Teal *anchored off the shore, we sat down on a pebbly beach to eat our supper. Suddenly we were fired on. Fortunately we made friends with the pranksters who were behind a boulder up a slope to the south, and they showed us the one well on the island, surrounded by a thicket and many mosquitoes. We all sat around drinking water from an old rusty cup, eight swarthy piratical characters, and Bob and I dreaming of the old fishing colony and cursing the government for using the island as a practice bombing and strafing range. Late that night aboard* Teal, *mosquitoes were drilling through our sleeping bags so we got sail on and put out. After nearly being run down by a PT boat in the early morning fog off Sow and Pigs lightship, we had a tasty breakfast of bacon, fried bread, and coffee cooked over the folding Sterno stove. That night we put into Cuttyhunk Harbor and rowed over to a neat little 28-foot sloop where the owner, a man of wonderful experience, loaned us pipe tobacco, and talked far into the night of his many voyages as crewmember and skipper of some famous vessels. Now retired, he was singlehandling the North American East Coast in his beautiful craft. We begged him to take us with him. He refused.*

When the summers ended, Bob and his mother would return to waterless Urbana, Illinois, to be with his father. During the school year Bob was expected to take riding, golf, and tennis lessons and sing in the choir. It was all a far cry from the ocean, but that didn't prevent him from studying pictures of old boats, drawing them, and making models as he tried to figure out what makes a boat and the water fit together.

Photographs: Personal collection.

High School

In 1945 Bob, now seventeen and a senior at Rindge Technical School in Cambridge, was required to write a senior thesis. He titled it *The Principles of Marine Architecture*.

Many years later, Peter Vermilya of Mystic Seaport read the paper and commented:

The major value of the paper is what it foretells of Bob the person. What he believed at age eighteen he seems to have believed all his life.

He thought that yacht design should be based on experience, his own and others. He steers clear of elaborate mathematical and scientific "proofs" for his points; rather, he uses practical explanations based on his own observations; observations which can be replicated by the average yachtsman. And that's the essence of science. When talking about rigging and sails, he doesn't go into aerodynamics of airfoils, etc., but instead dis-

cusses what combinations have worked in the past, for what reasons and under what conditions.

Bob had no formal training, but skillfully and surely developed his own design skills and principles. By the time he was twenty-two he had filled a workbook of over 200 designs and sketches: prams, skiffs, dinghies; sloops, ketches, schooners, square-riggers, barks, brigs, steamboats, and tugs.

He was drawing his information from real boats that appealed to him and incorporating the features into his own designs.

All of which is not to say that Bob disdained "Theory." He seems to have had use for it on an applied level—it was his handmaiden, not his goddess. (See Appendix II to read Bob's senior thesis)

Following high school, Bob spent nine months at Woods Hole Oceanographic laboratories serving as an able-bodied seaman. Near the end of the war, he entered the U.S. Army and served as an orthopedic mechanic, using his skilled hands to make braces and artificial limbs.

Photographs: Personal collection.

The Dragon Boat Shop

Discharged from the army in 1949, Bob knew he needed to get a job, even though deep in his blood ran a strain of stubborn opposition to the status quo, a will to reshape the world to his heart's desire—beautiful in shape and leisured in time, preferably cast in the eighteenth century when gaff-rigged boats and pipe-smoking were enough to let a man function. But dreams don't earn money. When he heard about an opening in the shop program at St. George's School, then a boy's prep school in Middletown, Rhode Island, Bob reluctantly went for an interview.

"Bob came in raw," said Norris (Norrie) Hoyt, English teacher and sailing instructor at the school, who was sitting in the headmaster's office that day. In no time Bob was hired to teach mechanical and engineering drawing. During the next six years he transformed what had been a typical prep school shop program—pencil holders and ashtrays to take home for Christmas—into an exciting and productive boatbuilding program. Bob named his shop the Dragon Boat Shop. He had sixteen students. "This was great good fun," he said. "I could design all kinds of little boats for the boys to build while they experimented with different construction methods."

During this time Bob and Norrie became close friends, and if it hadn't been for Norrie, who told me about those days, I would have known little about Bob's early small-boat designs and his teaching ability. "The boys," Norrie remembered, "liked the idea of building boats; from laying out on the lofting floor, picking up the lines, making the molds, and then actually building." Lumber began to pile up in corners, bills accumulated in the little room plastered to the wall of Baker's office; you could see east, west, and north from there, and it wasn't heated in winter. Mainly skin and bone as he was, he must have minded, but he loved the snug privacy while the kids were involved with boat projects as grandiose as they could muster or as simple as they liked. Meanwhile, in his little cube of a room, Bob was drawing boats, making delicious small models, smoking his pipe, and disapproving of the straight sheers and cramped underbodies of the latest development of the Sparkman & Stephens line."

One of the first Baker designs that the students built was the Dragonfly, a centerboard sloop with a planning hull that was cedar strip-planked for light construction. The boat had a 4-foot aluminum centerboard operated by a tricky mechanism that Bob invented. "You could move the centerboard fore and aft in order to perfect her sail-

Dragonfly
LOA: 20′0″; Beam: 6′0″

ing balance and even hoist out the centerboard for beaching the boat. "This," he said, "required a lot of very careful designing."

❖

Bob designed the Puddleduck with the students in mind. She was a sailing pram with a sliding gunter rig, to be built by the students and used in the school sailing program. Her size was determined because all that would be needed for each side was one 8-foot sheet of plywood. Thirty boats were built at the school. They sailed like a champion, responsive, very seaworthy, and fun to sail.

Norrie Hoyt remembered shoving the kids out in the Ducks,

with the tiller in one hand, and their elegant sails in the other:

*Some of them would find out what to do at once, a few would make it far-
ther out, cast loose the sheet, paddle with the rudder, and earnestly request
advice.*

*Baker would sail out, pipe in jaw, lank frame elegantly draped all
over the little boat, and nudge alongside the victim, suggesting as he
herded the helpless child that he pull in the sheet, pull the tiller toward
himself, let out the sheet a little, center the tiller, and as the sail took the
wind and the boat reached toward the shore, Baker would slide away
smiling complacently. This general air of secret wisdom had the effect of
letting the novices educate themselves and thus acquire critical instinct
and self-confidence."*

Puddleduck
LOA: 7'10³/₄"; Beam: 4'0"

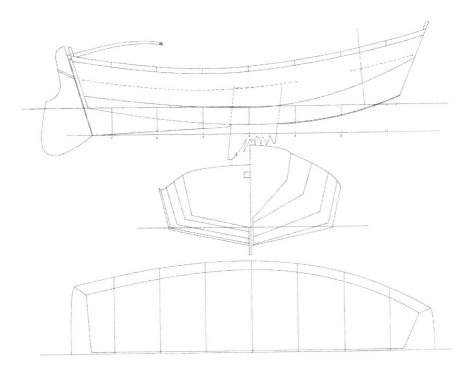

The Puddleduck was such a success that Bob's first wife, Anna, decided that they should mass-produce the boat. This meant of course, endless boat shows, regattas, production, marketing, and collecting. Bob, confused by ambition and flattery, resentful about being organized and advertised, found a splendid outlet for his frustration—he rebuilt an ancient fire engine to carry the Puddleducks hither and yon.

❖

The idea for the *Gosling* initiated with the loss of Norrie's dinghy during a hurricane. Bob, filled with enthusiasm, said, "I'll design a sailing dink that will beat everything and look like a boat, not a box."

Gosling
LOA: 9'6"; Beam: 4'3"

The *Gosling*'s construction would be double-diagonal with a sliding-gunter rig—a fast little yacht dinghy and also a class boat. They decided to build the first boat together.

Bob's first idea was that I, Norrie Hoyt, English instructor, should learn lofting. I volunteered to let Bob do it, but no. So I rented a floor sander and scuffed all the varnish off the floor of our dining room, first moving the table upstairs and taking the chairs to various inconvenient locations. Next, while Bob smoked at me, I laid out with steel tape, battens, and weights, all the lines of the Gosling, *and when completed, painted them in bright colors on the floor.*

Bob assured me that once the boat was built we could walk it out of the dining room, around the right angle and the radiator in the front hall, and out the door. I believed him. Nobody else did, and as the building progressed, the pile of Honduras mahogany strips, clamps, tools, the bucket of copper tacks, the bucket of copper washers, and the plans, filed up the corners of the room.

Finally planked and looking beautiful, Norrie and Bob had to go their separate ways for a few days. Returning, they found the dinghy, her building frame and all, in the front yard. Norrie's wife, Kitty, had had enough.

"Lured and encouraged by Bob's friendly stubbornness, Bob and I removed the boat from the building molds and carefully took it back into the house, this time through the front door originally intended for the exit. Nobody was looking. We put it back in the dining room." On Kitty's return, one piercing scream convinced them that the "Geese and the *Gosling*" better nest elsewhere! "We quickly exited the boat to the shop where we painted her in great style. "

"*Gosling* was beautiful: fast and stable. She sailed very well, doing just what she was designed for. I was quite pleased with her," Bob told me years later.

Bob believed in traditional methods and materials for boatbuilding and ultimately would return to them. In the meantime there was strip planking, diagonal planking, plywood, and a concocted material called fiberglass, suddenly appearing on the horizon.

Being of curious mind, even the plastic imposter had to be dealt with. In 1958, Bob designed his first fiberglass boat, the 10-foot Sprite. The design was to be a trainer for the school. Manned by a crew of two, or even three for interscholastic contests, as a trainer it could be a one-man boat first. This was accomplished by having two mast steps, a cat rig as a starter, and then promoting the kids to a

Sprite (Spirit)
LOA: 10'0"; Beam 4'7"

sloop rig, and finally, the addition of a spinnaker, giving the student definite objectives. Bob didn't have a traditional boat in mind. He wanted to design a very small boat where kids could sail safely and if they did it right they could plane the beast. And it worked! Bob said. "Scared the hell out of me the first time I planed her." Norrie remembered suggesting to Bob that he should sell the Sprite plans to a boat-building company. But Bob shied away. He didn't realize just how

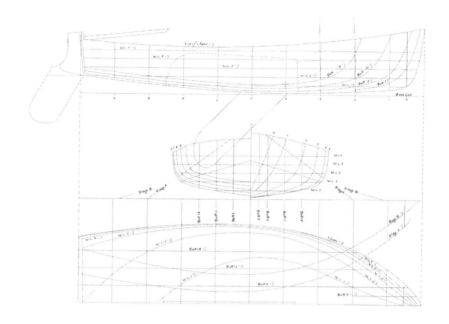

gifted he was as a designer but after much debate, he finally agreed to show the plans to George O'Day, owner of the O'Day Corporation, one of the first companies trying to create a market for little family boats rather than large racing sailboats. O'Day loved the Sprite and found Bob to be a meticulous designer.

The Sprite, much to Bob's surprise, was an instant success and after the first thousand were sold, he was still surprised. Thirty-five hundred were built before his royalties ran out.

Some of the boats Bob designed for O'Day, he never got into to see how they performed. "You get the satisfaction once you get it down on paper," Bob told Norrie. "You see it in its finished product, in its three dimensions. (In order for Baker Boat Works to later sell the Sprite's plans, her name was changed to Spirit.)

I was fascinated by Norrie's stories. Clearly, St. Georges brought together many elements of Bob's life. And like the learning place it was, it was a place I learned about Bob's early days before I knew him.

Contributions: Peter Vermilya. Norris Hoyt.
Photographs: Personal collection.

A Love Affair

While designing, teaching and building small boats at St. George's School, Bob's deeper interests were in the workingman's boat. An opportunity to further his interest arrived when he took a break from the school to get married.

Bob and his bride Anna had chosen to honeymoon on Martha's Vineyard, Massachusetts, an out-of-the-way island that Bob also knew would be an excellent place to look for workingmen's fishing boats.

Bob had an innate sense for scouting out working boats and while poking around Menemsha—the tiny harbor at the west end of the Vineyard, he found a maritime rarity and became involved in a second love affair.

Her name was *Orca*. Built in 1882, she was a Noman's Land boat, a boat steeped in tradition and all but a vanished breed.

The Noman's Land boats were named after the same small island five miles south of Martha's Vineyard where Bob had previously cruised. Because Noman's Land Island was close to the fishing grounds, it soon became the summer home for many of the Vineyard's fishermen and their families. During the Second World War, Noman's Land Island was seized by the government for use as target practice, and the families were forced to leave. Even today, parts of the island are off limits due to the possibility of unexploded bombs.

The Noman's Land boats were open, two-masted double-enders averaging 17 to 20 feet in length. Originally built as keel boats, by 1886 centerboards had been installed. Built with cedar and oak, the early boats were lapstrake but as time passed, they were more often carvel planked.

The sails were two loose-footed spritsails. The spars were light

and easily stowed in the boat when rowing Not only had the Noman's Land boats been developed for work in the same waters that Bob had lived beside and learned from, but he also knew their seaworthiness was well proven.

Two weeks later Bob and *Orca* left Menemsha with her bow pointed home on the long reach across Buzzard's Bay to Westport Point.

Orca had been a true workingman's boat with all the marks of her history etched in her hull. Bob studied each mark to understand how she had been used. He studied her construction and researched her history, He measured her, drew her lines, drew three perspective views of her hull to better understand her shape, and then compared her lines to existing Noman's Land half models on display at Mystic Seaport Museum.

Before Bob started restoring *Orca*, he made many inquiries about her history and her original rig. He wrote to Onslow S. Robinson, whose grandfather first owned the boat. When Bob received a reply from Robinson, *Orca*'s history, construction, and rig were confirmed.

It gives me great pleasure to know that my grandfather's boat has passed into the hands of one who appreciates her historical value. Orca *was built for my grandfather, Onslow Stuart, about 1882. I believe he entered small-boat fishing and lobstering shortly after he gave up whaling in 1850. The* hull was built by Delano at the Beetle yard in Fairhaven, Massachusetts. She was smooth planked instead of clinker built, and an indication of later construction. Grandfather took the hull home to his place in Chilmark, where he had a hinged partition between his barn and workshop so he could bring a boat as large as Orca through the barn doors and partly into the shop. There he installed the seats, deck, wash rail, and all the interior fittings to complete the boat.

The centerboard went alongside the keel - I believe it was on the starboard side. The fish well was unequally divided by the centerboard. The keel was quite narrow and had a keel iron about 1-foot square to facilitate hauling the boat up on skid ladders using oxen, as was done at Noman's Land and at Lobsterville, Menemsha. The oxen were hitched by short, heavy ropes and shackled to the pulling hole low on the stern. I believe you will find the forward mast band set in a heavily kneed piece still intact. The sternpost has been replaced, now heavier than original.

The forward sail was a relatively large gaff type without boom but frequently with club, a short 30-inch piece of wood to which the sheet was attached. The after sail was of the sprit type, probably without a boom in order to facilitate furling, as this mast and sail was frequently unstepped, either during a stiff breeze or during calm when rowing became necessary.

I last used the boat in 1920.
Onslow S. Robinson

Finally, when Bob felt he knew her inside out, he set about restoring her. Because *Orca* had been modified over the years, Bob carefully searched out old notches and holes in her construction in order to restore her centerboard case and thwarts to their original positions. The position for one thwart eluded him, but not wanting to assume its location, he left it out.

Onslow Robinson's description of *Orca*'s rig raised some questions for Bob. He had learned from his research that the islanders considered the boats to be "schooners," with foresail and main. The foremast and main were spritsail rigged, with the club on the main or after sail. "Chances are," Bob wrote, "that the club got 'innovated' about the second time the fellow in the after end got clobbered with the main boom."

Bob experimented with *Orca*'s rig and came up with a version

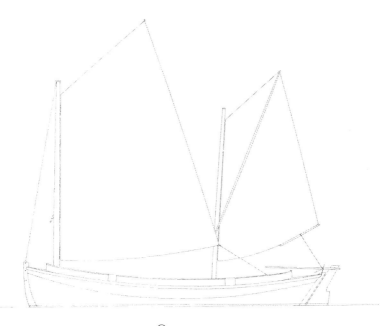

Orca
LOA: 19′9½″; Beam: 6′5½″
Measured and drawn by RHB

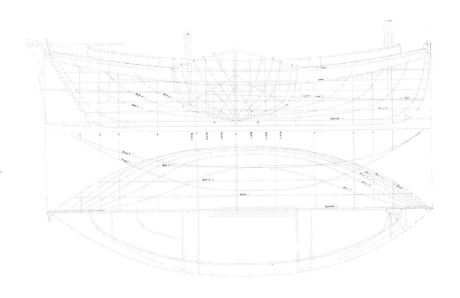

that, while it may not be completely original, worked well. The snotters for the sprit had double eyes and were long enough to allow the sprit to swing. Though the island people used a single sheet on the foresail, Bob rigged it double for singlehandling. He set up a mainsheet horse to for a better lead and to get the sheet out of the way of the tiller.

Working boats, Bob felt, should have their sailing performance judged with their intended task in mind—they were tools designed for a certain purpose.

"*Orca* sails well," Bob wrote, "but cannot be driven with her rail down or she will 'die.' When you put the helm down, she will go where you point her and not get hung up in the middle. The old horse handles just as she should—slowly but steadily."

❖

Another Noman's Land boat, known as "Cleveland's Noman's Land Boat," was acquired by Mystic Seaport in 1952, the same year Bob acquired *Orca*, but instead of being launched she was put on a cradle and trucked overland to Mystic. In 1972 Mystic hired Bob to research,

restore and prepare the
Cleveland's Noman's Land
Boat for exhibit. The boat
was the typical clinker-built
type and had been used for
codfishing in the waters surrounding the beaches of
Noman's Land. Her double
ends, like all Noman's Land

boats, were ideally suited for launching off the beaches through the
surf, then rowing to deep waters where the sails were set.

She was built by Captain Josiah Cleveland in 1882, and Bob
noted, "Both the Noman's Land boats, *Orca* and *Cleveland*, have definite similarities, close enough so that the two of them are obviously
the same model. They are both Delano-built boats; *Cleveland* used either Delano's half model or Delano's molds. In more recent years an
engine was installed in the *Cleveland* boat and her rig changed from a
two-masted spritsail to a single-mast gaff-rigged catboat."

Bob's work would involve stripping her to her original structure,
documenting, measuring, and taking off her lines. Again, Bob
learned much about the original boat by working from old photos of
the boat and details that he found in the structure. The photos proved
useful when it became obvious to Bob that the foredeck had been
cross-planked.

"There is only one set of fastening holes and these line up nicely
for the cross-planking shown in the photos. It is safe to assume the
back porch was cross-planked too, as there is just one crossbeam at
the bulkhead and signs of a strongback from the breasthook to the
beam."

After Bob studied the fish well, he went on to comment, "It seems
original, although the construction seems weak. I can't quite rational-
ize the well being cut off at the top, forward, and I question why
there is no fastening between the middle thwart and the case."

And, of course, some questions had no answers.

"There is something strange about the foremast step," he commented. "Three-quarters of it is obviously an old piece of wood. It's
been patched, but it appears to have been there for a good many

years. Yet two of the risers are replacements and the thing is hung down with iron screws. Why the peculiar cut in the top and the long slot with the carefully finished end? The after end appears to be a new cut. All remains a mystery."

The correct colors to paint a specific boat were important to Bob. After discovering what her original paint colors were, he went on to advise what the Noman's Land boat should look like.

"The deck and curbing should be white, in which case the sheer plank and both guards would be painted out a darker color. The hull looks a lot prettier before the lower guard is put on. It might be a good idea to paint the sheer plank a contrasting color, such as brick or barn red or green, including the lower guard. The upper guard and deck edge get a third color, yellow. White topsides, and inside a light, lead grey. I feel this boat was kept overboard for a long period, therefore a copper bottom might not be out of place, and it appears that the original home-brewed copper paint was green."

Thanks to Bob's inquisitive mind, thoroughness, and dedication, future generations may look at these two Noman's Land boats, now on permanent display at Mystic Seaport, and from their appearance form some kind of mental picture of the amphibious generations of coastal men and women. (Bob ultimately donated *Orca* to Mystic Seaport Museum.)

Contributions: Peter Vermilya, Mystic Seaport.
Photographs: *Orca,* personal collection; Cleveland Noman's Land Boat, Mystic Seaport.

Commonsense Boats

Orca had opened the gates, and from this point on "commonsense boats," as Bob called them, became his life's passion. Although there were many of these small craft working the waters for the Newport lobster and hook-and-line industries, it was so long ago that the importance of the Newport fish and lobster boats had been superseded by the Newport catboat.

It was 1953 when Bob, still teaching at St George's School, became interested in the Newport fish and lobster boats, Newport cats, the Newport shore boats, and a pulling boat named *Rescue*.

Bob had a good friend and kindred spirit when it came to talking old boats, the late John H. Benson of Newport, Rhode Island. Benson had a great interest in the early Newport boats. In addition, Benson owned a Newport cat named *Penguin,* built in 1885 by Thomas Stoddard and purchased by Benson in 1934.

Benson's wife's family had owned the *Kingfisher I*, built in 1872 (no longer in existence but well documented and photographed), and at the time owned *Kingfisher II*, built in 1895. These provided a magnificent wealth of old stuff for Bob's curious mind.

The Newport cats began to appear in the 1860s and by 1885 the traditional lapstrake construction of the earlier Newport fish and lobster boats had been replaced by smooth planks, the deep keel replaced by a centerboard, the bottom showing some rocker and with more curve to the forefoot. There was an increase in beam, the narrow washboards were replaced by a half-deck, and the lower guardrail was removed. The mainmast was stepped directly through the deck. The only significant rig change, however, was a slightly higher peak on the gaff, and a headsail was no longer used.

The final transition to a Newport cat can be seen in the 17-foot *Kingfisher II*. Bob commented, "The one thing that the Newport

Penguin
A Newport Catboat
LOA: 16'6"; Beam: 10'⁵/₈"
Measured and drawn by RHB

boats had in common were heavy quarters, which seems to be typical Newport, and I wonder if it's a hindrance. Obviously, what the builder-designers had in mind was to hold the quarters up for a load."

Although, *Penguin* and *Kingfisher II* had been rebuilt, the shapes of their hulls had not changed. To a layman they looked identical, but Bob knew them to be quite different.

"To anyone who really didn't look," he said, "they looked like the same damn boat. The fact of the matter is that they are dramatically

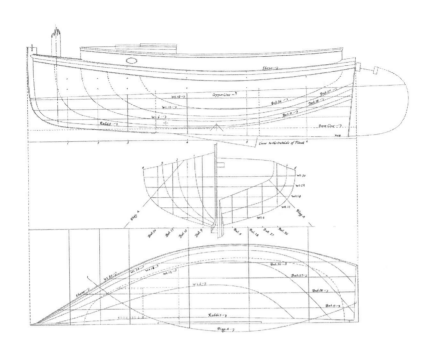

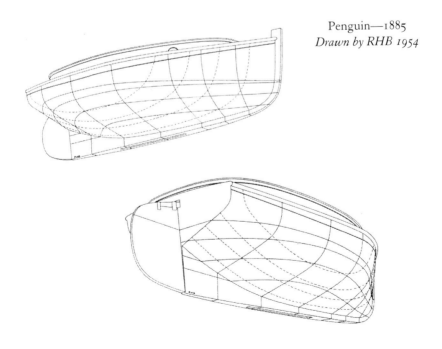

Penguin—1885
Drawn by RHB 1954

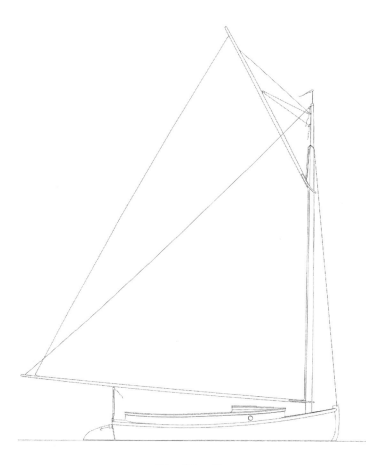

Kingfisher II
LOA: 16' 11½"; Beam: 8' ½"
Measured and drawn by RHB

different." *Penguin* has a lot more deadrise. She is plum-stemmed
with a deep forefoot and sharp entrance—a workingman's boat.
Kingfisher II was a leisure man's boat."

To clarify his thoughts about the differences in the two boats, he
measured and drew their lines. From these lines he drew a perspective of both hulls for comparison and as a means of honing in on his
perceptions. Bob had the ability to see and understand shape, a skill
that few people achieve, and this art of perception is what guided him
all his life.

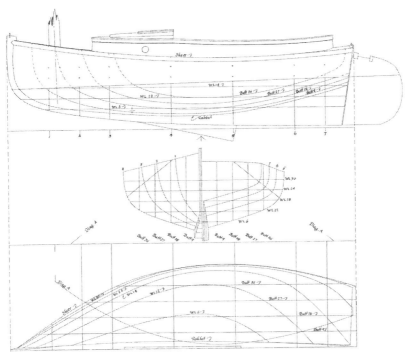

Kingfisher II—1895
Drawn by RHB 1954

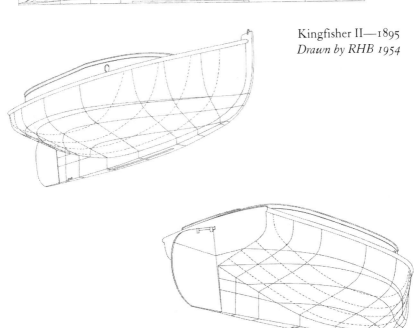

Finding a Way with Lettering

John Howard Benson, in addition for his love for workingmen's boats, was a graphic artist, stone carver, author, educator at the Rhode Island School of Design, and a well-known calligrapher. As such, Benson was disturbed by Bob's handwriting on his designs and sketches.

"The lines of your boat designs are inked beautifully," he told Bob, "but your handwriting is atrocious." With that said, Benson handed Bob his book, *Elements of Lettering,* and said, "Fix it."

And he did. By 1955 and forever after, Bob's beautiful handwriting graced his elegant drawings, letters he wrote, notes he pinned up on the fridge, and even the weekly market list.

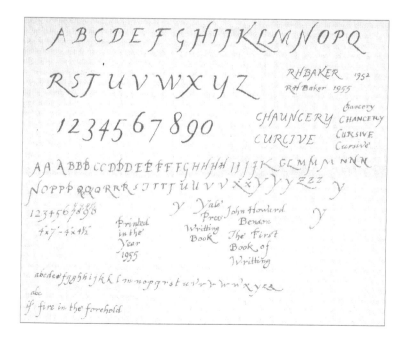

abcdefghijklmnopqrstuvwxyz ʒ

of which abceghijklmnoqrsuvwz
are made in one stroke. That is, a ↙start here. b l

Further, d f p t x y are made with two strokes.
As: d f p t x v

A A B C D E E F F G G H I J J J K L L M N N ·
O P Q R S T T U V W X Y Z

Capital letters should be formed almost
straight up and down ↕ A A H ·

Small letters can lean just a little: ↗ l l l l h.

Some letters can be joined to others. ai ti ts st ct
er mi ni in im ir stir and others.

Fancy Letters Should Be Left

Alone For awhile.
    1234567890   1234567890
        1981   So should fancy
        1979
                            Numbers !

Robert Baker
Westport Point
February 1958

An Auction

During the St. George's School's summer break in 1953, Bob attended an auction in Sakonnet, Rhode Island, where the contents of a house and barn were to be sold. Stowed in a dusty, dark corner of the barn was a small boat that looked ancient. Bob's instincts told him it was important, and thirty dollars later he owned her, took her home, and for his own archives felt compelled to take off her lines and document her construction. With the plans safely stored in his archives, he didn't have money enough to restore her so he donated her to Mystic Seaport.

The Seaport gave it a coat of paint and for lack of any particular identification referred to it as the Sakonnet River boat because of where Bob had found her.

The origin of the boat continued to puzzle Bob. Finally he stumbled across a series of old photographs showing a whole bunch of little fishing boats that closely resembled the boat he had found.

The location in the photographs was easily identified by the old stone boathouse situated at the foot of Ledge Road in Newport. From the dress of the men in the photographs and the types of horse-drawn carriages, Bob deducted that the photos were taken around 1860 to 1870.

He felt some of the boats were older types than others. One had a heart-shaped transom that resembled a ship's yawlboat. Another was a double-ender with a sculling hole cut into a crotch and nailed to the sternpost. A third had an oval transom. But they were all about the same length, 11 feet, with a beam under 5 feet, plus two common characteristics: heavy quarters and sharp entrances.

When Bob bought the boat at auction it had no rig, spars, or rudder, but the gudgeons were still intact, indicating that the boat had been steered with a rudder. Bob felt that these boats were probably rigged with a spritsail because of its ease in handling.

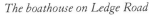

The boathouse on Ledge Road

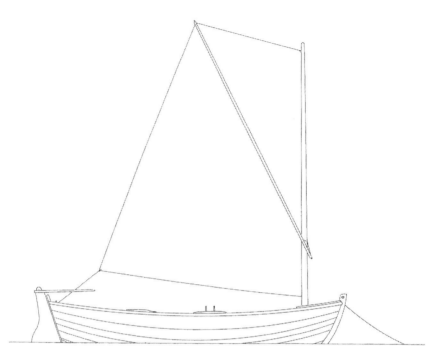

Newport ShoreBoat (Sakonnet River Boat)
LOA: 11′4 ¾″; Beam: 7′7 ½″
Measured and drawn by RHB

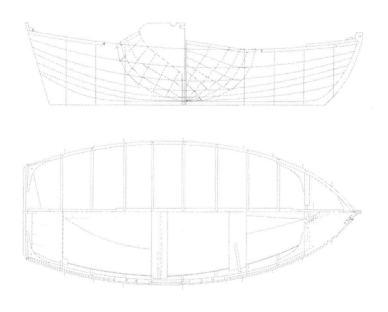

Some of the photos showed the rig lying in the boat, but there were none of the boats under sail. The boats had no centerboards and the keels were not deep enough to provide windward ability, but they would be excellent at downwind sailing, a real help at the end of the day with a full load of fish. Otherwise they were rowed or sculled. "Their fine entrance and run would make sculling easy and fast," Bob explained.

After careful study of these photos and a comparison of the lines he had taken, Bob was convinced the "Sakonnet River boat" was the only known survivor of a distinct and separate type that existed only in Newport.

Then one day Bob examined a painting of the nineteenth-century yacht *America* in Irish waters. Anybody with him would have assumed he was looking at the yacht, but knowing Bob, he would be looking at the little workboats that, like pilot fish, were surrounding the big yacht. That's when he noticed a small boat in the foreground that looked exactly like the Sakonnet River boat. It all came together as additional research unfolded, revealing that the Irish had immigrated to Newport as early as 1840 to work as masons building the mansions on Bellevue Avenue. This meant that the boats on Ledge Road were direct descendants of the traditional Irish small boat he'd seen in the painting, having been built by Irish immigrants and used for fishing when work was slack.

Thanks to Bob's stubborn research the boat that he bought at auction was finally identified and is the only known survivor of those little boats on Ledge Road. Bob restored her for Mystic Seaport and her name, Sakonnet River boat, has been corrected to Newport Shore boat.

The 1950s were a thrilling but hard time for Bob. He never spoke directly about his driving curiosity and need to see things as they were, and not use someone else's interpretation. While finding his true direction, his family was still expecting something different from him. "Don't forget," his mother would say, "President Franklin Roosevelt was your godfather." Fortunately, in the meantime, he met naval architect and maritime historian Howard Chapelle and got a needed boost when Chapelle asked Bob to come and work for him. Bob toyed with the idea but turned it down. Bob remained true to himself, despite the opposition from family and friends. I shudder to think what might have happened to Bob's inquisitive mind if he had gotten swallowed in the framework of an organization.

Photographs: Personal collection.

Fiberglass

Due to the continuing success of the Sprite, Bob was getting inquiries from other production boatbuilders—just what he needed as his research was earning him satisfaction but little money.

In 1960, Tom Bigelow, who had worked for O'Day as a salesman, decided to start his own boatbuilding business in Warwick. Rhode Island. He named his new company Sailstar Boats. Impressed with Bob's designs and looking for rapid growth, Bigelow called Bob and explained that he wanted a boat a little bigger than the Sprite. From Bob's drafting table appeared the Little Bear.

The Tallstar was another success, and the next boat Bob designed for Bigelow in 1961 was the 19-foot Orion.

Little Bear
LOA: 11'6"; Beam: 4'9"

With the success of these boats, Sailstar Boats grew very fast but without profit. In 1967, Bigelow sold Sailstar Boats and moved to Warren, Rhode Island, where he started a new place called Talman Yacht Company. This time Bigelow was thinking bigger: a cruising boat that was also pretty to look at and reflected some of the beauty and romance of earlier New England sailing craft.

After talking with Bob, they both agreed that the Muscongus Bay sloop, a sailing workboat, could esthetically and economically combine traditional boatbuilding materials with fiberglass.

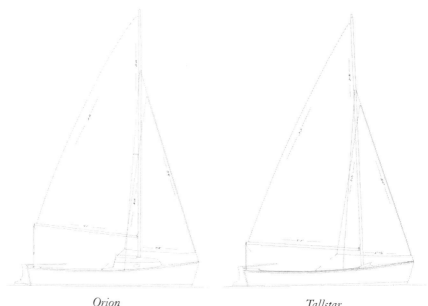

Orion
LOA: 19′0″; Beam: 6′9″

Tallstar
LOA: 14′0″; Beam: 5′9 ½″

From Bob's drawing board came the Menemsha 24 followed by the Katama, the same basic hull and interior layout as the Menemsha but with a lengthened bow and slightly higher rig. Both the Menemsha and the Katama had either mahogany or teak trim.

Bob was satisfied with this transition from a classic design to modern materials and requirements, but deep down, he was not that pleased with the idea of fiberglass. Of all the materials, the concept of fiberglass was the most alien to Bob. Not a wood, it represented something false, a threat to the comfortable association of man and boat. He enjoyed the experiment, but boating for Bob meant finding some quiet spot up the Westport River in an old wooden boat.

Photographs: Talman Bigelow.

Menemsha
LOA: 24′2″; Beam: 8′0″

A Telephone Call

It was a warm spring day in 1961 when I answered the phone. The man on the other end asked for Pete. "That's me," I replied (it was my enduring childhood nickname). "How can I help you?" He said his name was Bob Baker and that he had been told I had a barn full of antique house parts for sale. "I'm looking for an old mantel for a house I'm designing for a client," he said.

I assured him that rescuing old house parts was my business, and that I had an extensive collection. We arranged an appointment for the following week. Innocent enough, until a week later at 10 a.m., when he knocked on my door. His shiny black hair lay like a mane over his chiseled features, and his eyes, the color of jade, contrasted nicely with the blue scarf flung casually around his shoulders. As the smoke from his stubby pipe gave out a delicious aroma, my eyes dropped down to his canvas coat with elbow patches and his leather moccasins—scuffed with the patina of time. He was gorgeous—like an explorer who had just returned from an exotic adventure. And when he removed his pipe and grinned, there was no need for "hello"; it was if we had always known each other, and I knew my life was about to change.

I can't remember how we got to the barn or even how I managed to sell him some woodwork. Bob, too, was a collector. He was mainly a marine architect but also diddled with houses. I learned that his main passion was designing, collecting, and studying small water-craft, but that didn't exclude a collection of old cars, a set of narrow-gauge trains he had built, and even some old house parts. We kept discovering each other and how nicely we fit together, and before he left I agreed to meet him at an old house he wanted to show me, and then of course there were the boats. We spent hours wandering through boatyards, marshes, and on the shores looking for derelicts—

sailboats, rowing boats, workboats—to photograph, measure, or save. And in between there were derelict eighteenth-century houses to explore, and over the next few months our relationship became solid. I had discovered a way to be me in combination with another

A year later my husband agreed to a divorce. Bob and I moved in together. Eventually my five kids (Bob's two children, by his marriage to Anna, were living in England) went back and forth between our house and their father's, except our house by then was a boat named *Kalmia*.

A Pinky

When I think of Bob's deep interest in workingmen's boats, I think of a day when we were on our way to Maine to see his friend and collaborator, Lance Lee, when suddenly he turned onto a side road. "I want to show you something," he said. I didn't need to ask what.

We parked and walked across a marsh. At the edge, nestled in the salt grass, were the weathered bones of a rotting hull. "That's the Prospect Marsh pinky," Bob said.

I was new at this boat-identifying game and all I could see was rotting wood. But being beside Bob, it wasn't long before I saw how magical this hull was—a hull that he could read simply by looking at it, a hull that spoke to him, and through Bob's eyes, spoke to me.

When Bob started to collect some of her bones lying in the tall marsh grass nearby, it was clear he loved this boat. As he carefully stowed the bones into his backpack, he explained her history. He told me that in 1937 Lincoln Colcord first discovered this abandoned pinky on the shores of Prospect Marsh in Maine. Colcord told his friend Howard Chapelle about his discovery. Both men knew that this was a pinky, an offshore fishing vessel identified by a schooner rig and narrow stern that rose upwards like a tombstone. It was a type of boat that had been noted as early as 1760, but was now a dying breed. Although this pinky had been sitting in the marsh grass for at least twelve years, she was together enough for Chapelle and Colcord to take off a set of lines.

In the 1950s when Chapelle arrived at Bob's shop with a rolled-up set of plans of this pinky. Bob was particularly impressed with the details that Chapelle and Colcord had so carefully noted: the rudder head; the back porch, as Bob called it; the sawn frames; double stanchions; etc. "To bother with the details is something rare to find," Bob said. And naturally he had gone to Maine to see the boat for himself.

Perserverance
LOA: 26′2 ½″; Beam: 9′2″
Measured and drawn by RHB

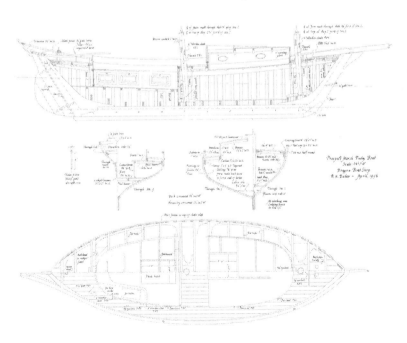

Bob loved that boat and couldn't resist redrawing her lines—perhaps to understand her better and squeeze out more of her life by studying every line. Without changing her hull shape, Bob added to the plans by including a deck, interior accommodations, and rigging.

Years later, Bob showed the plans to Lance Lee, director of the Apprenticeshop in Rockland, Maine. Lee also had seen the same pinky as a derelict, and he too had fallen in love with her remains. He was thrilled when he saw Bob's plans and knew the Apprenticeshop had to build the boat.

By 1984 the replica pinky, now properly named *Perseverance*, was launched and featured at the Newport, Rhode Island, WoodenBoat Show.

Lee commented, "She is a joy to handle. She has the feel of a little ship. She lies down slowly and not very far and slides for her destination. She is so extraordinarily graceful. She feels so reassuring, so competent, so wonderfully sure of herself."

Perseverance's home is still in Rockland and she's now owned by Lance's son Bjorn. I have heard Bob say many times, "Never pass up a rotting hull. It could be important."

Contributions and photographs: Lance Lee.

California

After three months of backbreaking labor on *Kalmia,* we had removed the worst of the blanket of scum and seaweed, above and below decks, most of the peeling paint, repaired the salon windows and erased the fish cartoon from the smokestack. From here on the work would be straightforward: engine overhaul, wood repair, sand, paint, and varnish.

Bob, still anxious to get to California, declared, "Now is the perfect time." Bob was determined to compare nineteenth-century design and construction methods between small craft built on the East Coast with those built on the West Coast.

During the 1850s, the vigorous whaling industry in San Francisco had attracted boatbuilders from New England hoping to profit from a demand for yawlboats, whaleboats, Whitehalls, and launches. Consequently, many New England boatbuilders migrated to the Bay to get in on the action. That included the Beetle family (boatbuilders from New Bedford, Massachusetts) and Kneiss from Connecticut. Bob knew this meant that virtually the same boats would have been built on both the East and West Coasts. Left behind on the West Coast would be East Coast boat designs, building skills, individual trademarks, and characteristics. This trip would provide a rare opportunity to compare the work of East and West Coast builders, so Bob imagined.

Not only was Bob's research on hold because of *Kalmia,* but also our baby was due in September. We expected to be gone for six months, and Frank agreed to keep an eye on the boat. Relieved, we bought some heavy nylon line and secured *Kalmia* against the blustery winds of New England's winter. *Kalmia* was taken care of but not *Orca,* which was innocently swinging back and forth on her mooring in the Westport River. Bob didn't want to store her on dry

land, and decided that the only solution was to donate her to Mystic Seaport with the condition that they keep her in the water. Mystic was delighted. Bob would miss her, but was relieved to know she was in good hands. With *Kalmia* and *Orca*'s futures resolved, we headed west.

Our Volvo station wagon and 10-foot Sprite lashed to a boat trailer were packed with the necessaries for an undetermined length of time exploring: clothes, music, books, tools, drafting material, and even darkroom equipment A few hours on the road would indicate how well our assorted paraphernalia would ride.

Driving across the country is usually considered straightforward Interstate highway stuff, but not with "rural route Bob" as navigator. As we crossed the country looking for old roads near lakes, ponds, rivers, we covered as many miles backward as forward. The Hudson River and Erie Canal were investigated and then the lower tip of the Great Lakes. On reaching the southern tip of Lake Erie we noticed a dirt lane named Water Road, surely a road worth investigating. Bumping down the lane, we came across an ancient sign "Boats For Rent" leaning against a sailboat that looked just as ancient. We stopped, looked at the boat, and then walked to the nearby house. Knocking on the door, we were welcomed by a hunchbacked, furrowed-faced man with a Santa Claus beard that reached to his waist. We asked him about the boat parked in his front yard. "Oh that," he said as if he had forgotten it was there. "Come, I'll show you." We followed as he limped to a barn and opened a door that had been shuttered for half a century. Inside at least twenty identical pulling boats were stacked one on top of another, each with their builder's plate, "Lyman Boat Works, Sandusky, Ohio. 1904."

"Yup," he said, "With Lake Eire next door, renting small rowing boats used to be quite a business a time a 'go. Wanta' buy one?"

Even though they were dried out, and without a doubt would sink at the first taste of water, we said yes. It was easy to imagine those early boaters in blue flannel pants, white shirts with red stripes, sideburns, bow ties, ladies in ankle-length dresses, leg-of-mutton sleeves, parasols, and straw hats.

Picking the best of the lot, we moved the Sprite off the trailer, loaded the Lyman, and headed for the railroad station. After uploading her onto the platform, we wrapped her in cardboard, filled out the paperwork, and sent a telegram to Frank, "*Kalmia*'s tender arriving by freight. Please pick up."

As usual, if Bob found an old boat that he knew was important, he either took photographs, took its lines, or it ended up in our backyard.

Fortunately for a compulsive boat collector there was a long stretch of waterless plains ahead, so instead of searching out boats, we looked for old silver mines. Looking in our AAA tour book, Bob discovered that there was an abandoned silver mine named Love, a

Lyman
LOA: 15'0"; Beam: 4'0"

town only a few hours out of our way. Following the AAA directions was like following a grid drawn in the sand. After two hours, with our lungs filled with dust and our clothes sticking like flypaper, we came to a crossroad and a faded sign that said, "Love. Population one. Twenty miles." The arrow pointed west, and within thirty minutes we had reached the foothills and entrance to the silver mine. Like a western movie-set, we found a single dirt road, rutted and narrow, bordered by a bank, a jail, a barroom, hotel and stable, all abandoned and collapsing. For a moment I thought about looking inside a building, but the quiet was deafening and the site spooky as a ghost town, which I agreed it was. Slowly cruising up the road, we suddenly dead-ended at house with a fresh coat of paint and a man standing on the porch.

I waved at the man and thought, okay that's population one. He waved back with a gun. Dead-ended in front of a gun, with car and boat trailer and nowhere to turn around, was like being caught without any clothes on. Bob backed and filled, backed and filled, while I kept smiling and nodding my head at what I was sure was an outlaw until finally the car and trailer were reversed. Retreating with a gun at one's back was a new experience. Go fast or go slow were our only options. Fast, we agreed. There was no love here. Stopping at the next town we asked about Love and the silver mine. Stay away, we were told. The man living there thinks everybody is after his mining claim and will stop at nothing to protect it.

Having our fill of the American frontier, we headed for the Pacific. It was late August by the time we arrived in San Francisco. After a stay in Sausalito to ferret out ancient derelicts recycled as houseboats, we decided to move to a little town called Inverness located at Point Reyes, a peninsula on Tomales Bay, an hour north of San Francisco. Our baby was due in four weeks and we were still living out of a suitcase; it was time to move to a more permanent place.

Little did we know that a combination of circumstances was about to offer us an excellent opportunity for small-boat research.

The final road to Inverness paralleled Tomales Bay. The area was remote with an innocent bygone look. The houses were simple, their inviting ribbons of chimney smoke reminiscent of a New England village. As we passed through the village I noticed what looked to be

an abandoned building sitting in the bay one hundred feet from shore. The faded letters painted across her roof spelled, out "Boats for Hire." I yelled, "Stop!" Bob shrugged his shoulders and kept going. Then conceding to a female hunch, he stopped and backed up. The walkway that led to the building was dilapidated and impassable. We waded out, and Bob hoisted me up so I could look in a window. I looked, then looked back at him. "Whoopee, pay dirt!" I yelled, "It's filled with old wooden boats."

Finding the owner wasn't difficult. Everybody knew Brock Schreiber. He lived in a small cottage built on the side of a hill with a postcard view of Tomales Bay. When we arrived he was sitting on his porch cocooned in a wicker chair. He looked to be in his eighties— his furrowed face and entwined body content and relaxed—he was at ease with the passing of time. Welcoming us with a nod he pointed to some chairs and asked us to sit down. "You're from out of town. I can tell by your accent," he said. We told him yes, that we came from Massachusetts in order to research small boats. "You've come to the right place," he said. And as he recounted the history of Inverness and its waterfront activity, we were slowly carried back to the nineteenth century. "Back then," he said, "Inverness was a resort village, busy with campers and vacationers who came to take advantage of the Tomales Bay waters."

By 1915, Brock, with his knowledge of boats and boatbuilding, had established a boat livery that rented boats to the tourists. "A lively

business," he said, "but at the start of the Second World War, I had to close down." The doors had been shut and the treasures locked away for twenty-two years, and this was exactly what we were looking for.

We talked on about his boats, while slowly gaining his trust. When we asked if we could go inside his boathouse he agreed to lend us a key. By the time we left, the sun had slipped into the Bay and the key had slipped into Bob's pocket. He hung on to it tightly as we gaily two-stepped up the road to our rented house. After unpacking our belongings, we set out a camera, rulers, paper and the key. We were ready for whatever the boathouse had to offered.

The building was indeed a museum, with little boats and related artifacts jammed to the rooftop. In addition to yawlboats, pulling boats, skiffs, and a launch, there were old paint and hardware catalogs, hand tools, sails, oars, and assorted boat paraphernalia, including a stationary gas engine that Brock told us he had used to drive his machinery.

We had discovered enough research material to last a lifetime. We felt like it was Valentine's Day, picking through a box of assorted chocolates. Realizing the importance of the collection, we contacted the San Francisco Maritime Museum. These boats should have been of interest to their curator, but his lack of curiosity was as dead-ended as a message in a bottle floundering in a back-eddy.

Our house, just down the street, gave us a chance to visit Brock often, talk about his boats, swap stories, and establish his confidence.

Finally he gave us our own key, and with it permission to use the shop as we wished with one condition: repair the walkway.

It was difficult to decide which boats were the most important to photograph, measure, and draw. An inventory of the shop included, among other things, eleven yawlboats, of which two had wineglass transoms. Brock referred to them as workboats or tenders used by the ferryboats that laid the Atlantic Cable, circa 1860. Research confirmed that one of these yawlboats was a tender used by the scow schooners in San Francisco Bay. Bob felt the boats were the work of three distinct builders or shops, with the Beetle shop having turned out two of the hulls. We took a set of lines off a 13-footer and dubbed her *Gray Boat*.

Instead of identifying his boats by name, Brock used numbers. The gray boat, number 16, was built circa 1880, and was representative of the remaining yawlboats. She was measured, photographed, and Bob drew up her lines.

Numbers 17, 18, and 19 were copies. "When a boat wore out I'd build a new one," Brock told us. Numbers 18 and 19 (left to right

Gray Boat
LOA: 13'3"; Beam: 4'10"
Measured and drawn by RHB

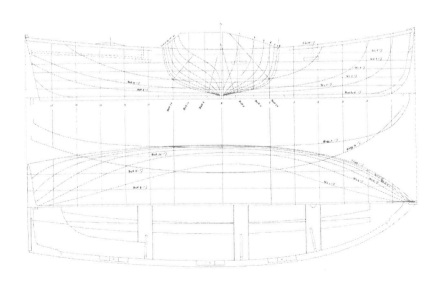

above) seemed in the best condition, so we restored them enough to test their performance. The trials proved interesting. These boats, heavy and difficult to row, were indeed built to work, and I felt sorry for the tourists who had come for a relaxing Sunday outing.

But the best old-boat find was about to happen. One day when walking home from the post office, I spotted a wineglass transom poking out from under a porch; I never would have seen it if the light hadn't been just right. Excited, I knocked on the door; I had definitely caught the old-boat disease.

"Camp here," a slurred voice said. And the door opened.

A disheveled man, waving a rum bottle, appeared. "Woops" was all I could think when I saw his matted beard, torn shirt, and blood-shot eyes. But he didn't look dangerous so I asked him about the boat under his porch. He flinched, "Oh my soul," he said, " there's a boat under there?" And I began to wonder which one of us was hallucinating

"Take a look," he said, raining my face with spittle, "and let me know."

I crawled under his porch, and took a quick survey to make sure there was more than just a transom. Not only was she all together, she was a Whitehall begging to be put back in the water. I offered Camp twenty-five dollars. "A deal," he said, waving his bottle and drenching my shirt in rum. Between swigs, Camp agreed to keep the boat until Bob's birthday two weeks later. Although another boat was not

what we needed, I was exhilarated by
my find, until I began to worry. What
if Camp stumbled and passed out for
good, or maybe claimed he didn't remember me, or even worse, that it
wasn't his boat? How could I have forgotten to get a receipt? Bob's birthday
had to be declared immediate. We
hitched up our trailer, pulled it down
to Camp's house and hauled the boat
out. She was 15 feet of beauty—a real
Whitehall designed for speed. A taxi of
the 1890s. She had sails, spars, oars, and
even had her name, *Azulykit,* carved
into her backrest.

Somehow boats were falling into
our lap, each one more lovely, it
seemed, than the previous. *Azulykit*
was now at the top of the list as tender
for *Kalmia*. We stripped off all her
paint, repaired a section of her transom

that had been removed for an outboard, replaced cracked frames, and caulked and painted her topsides with traditional Baker colors: white topsides, blue sheer plank, and a French-gray interior.

When launched, she proved a joy to row. With each pull on the oars, she slipped through the water with barely a ripple.

Sailing her was something else, for me, at least. She was spritsail-rigged and difficult to convince to come about. But not for Bob—he could handle her as if they were dancing the waltz together.

Photographs: Personal collection.
Azulykit has been donated to Mystic Seaport.

Azulykit
LOA: 14′ 11 ½″; Beam: 4′ 2 3/8″
Measured and drawn by RHB

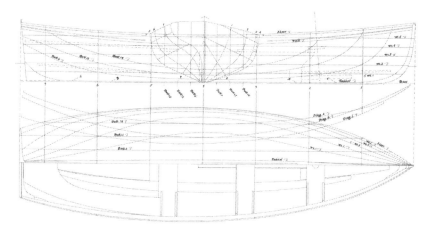

In late September our son Ben was born, but this didn't deter us from spending many hours in Brock's shop. While Ben slept in a basket, we measured and photographed the boats, and sorted through the tools, catalogs, and odd junk. Lunch breaks were declared, "explore time."

We'd head for local boatyards and inlets to search for more old boats. Bodega Bay, an inlet at the north end of Tomales Bay—a big hole in the coast, Bob called it—had been a popular place for large

Coos Bay Wherry
LOA: 11'2"; Beam: 3'4"
Measured and drawn by RHB

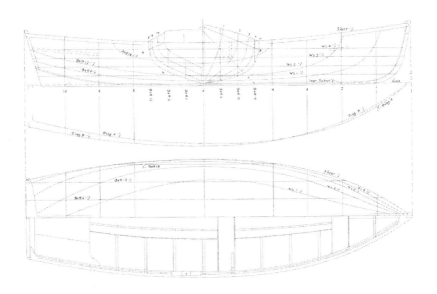

ships to lay over between trips, and a likely area to find abandoned small boats. In no time we found a lovely little rowing boat lying near a beach. Bob called her a Coos Bay wherry. She was lapstrake and lightly built, but not in good enough condition to row. We were able to measure and photograph her and take her lines, however. Further research revealed that she had been built in Coos Bay, Oregon, in 1925.

❖

In the evenings, after cataloging the day's finds, Bob worked on the design for a gaff-rigged pocket schooner and was close to finishing when we met Sam Guild in a hardware store. Sam and his wife, Anne, were natives of Maine but recently had moved to Marshall, a small town on Tomalas Bay across from Inverness. Naturally, two pairs of New Englanders living on Tomales Bay were bound to find each other—particularly because Sam was a boatbuilder.

We asked them over for dinner. While I cooked, Anne talked, and Sam looked at Bob's lines for the schooner.

"That's exactly what I want to build for myself," I heard Sam say. Sam bought the plans, built her back in Maine, and named her *Samanthe*. She was so perfectly proportioned that seen at a distance she appeared to be much larger than 28 feet. Bob was delighted the first time he went for a sail. "She is graceful, sails very well, is close-winded, and tacks close as many schooners don't."

Bob designed many boats but always with a traditional shape. For instance, if he were designing a cutter, he would know what the rig had to be, and how the boat had to sit in the water. He'd start with the sheer plan followed by a broadside view than worked up her details until he knew she was pretty, while all the time considering the specific requirements for her specific waters. Not until Bob was pleased with his design would he then go to work on the interior details.

Once a boat was designed, Bob felt strongly that changing its size was a risky proposition since its proportions would be lost; it was important to him that the design be a marriage with the water and the sky.

When I asked Bob why all his boat designs look like Baker boats, He replied, "It's the sheer and the shape of the ends, or maybe because I've been drawing the same damn boat shape for the last forty years."

Maynard Bray commented, "Bob, more than most people, had a real feel for the way old-time builders and boat designers understood that proportion, shape, and simplicity have everything to do with grace and beauty."

Samanthe
LOA: 27'8 ½"; Beam: 9'4 ½"

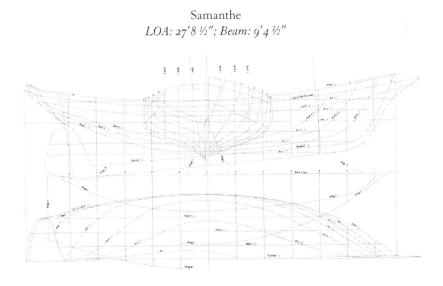

Living with a person who constantly thought about boats meant finding delicious little sketches in the bathroom, bedroom, kitchen, the telephone book, on the back of envelopes, on the market list and sales slips. Many grew into small models and meant that dusting was out of the question.

One of these models became the Widgeon, a sloop design for George O'Day. Trim, fast, and lightweight, yet roomy and stable, she could be sailed either as a sloop with a spinnaker or jib or with mainsail alone. The Widgeon is still very popular forty-some years later.

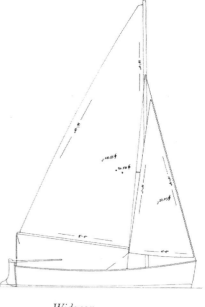

Widgeon
LOA: 12'0"; Beam: 5'0"

Sunk Again

January 1965 arrived, and with the New Year, a letter from Frank Northup. "*Kalmia* has sunk! A freak storm," he wrote. "Her lines stretched and a piling pounded a hole in her side. What do you want me to do? "

"Raise her," we replied, "We'll be back in the spring"—words that sealed our future with *Kalmia*.

Heading east was a bit more complicated. We now had a baby and three additional boats. Brock had given us #19, there were *Azu-lykit* and our 10-foot Sprite, plus a new collection of old tools, various other newly acquired treasures that could not be left behind, and all the original gear we had arrived with. We hired a moving van and at the last moment we shoved in the trailer, just to be on the safe side. We had enough boats for the moment.

When we had reached the halfway point of the 3,000-mile trip between California and Rhode Island, we began to notice that passersby were staring at us with ugly looks. All we could imagine was perhaps our Volvo had a wobbly tire or a loose door, but that was never the case. Finally, nearing the East Coast, we stopped at an out-of-the-way boatyard. Getting out of the car to look around, we were accosted by the boatyard owner. "Get out of here," he yelled. "We don't want hippies around here." So that was what all the staring had been about. Bob had grown a beard. It was a gorgeous new beard, but, we discovered, was threatening to people afraid of hippies.

It was spring when we arrived in Rhode Island and yes, it's true, the last few miles are the hardest. What would *Kalmia* look like? How much new damage? Why did we even buy her? As we approached Rhode Island, the sweet smell of awakening lilacs couldn't erase our uneasiness. We only knew that Frank had raised *Kalmia*, repaired the hole in her hull, pumped her out, and started the engines

to flush out the salt water. Beyond that, only our arrival would reveal what Frank hadn't, couldn't, or wouldn't tell us. To lessen our anxiety, we reviewed the work we had done on *Kalmia* before leaving for California. "She can't possibly be that much worse" Bob said, trying to bolster our spirits.

Frank greeted us timidly with a dismal look, dampening our small bit of hope. Walking down the dock, our worst fears were realized. *Kalmia*, listing at her berth, was scarred and broken. I was disheartened and feared that stepping aboard would bring greater sorrow and an unwelcome reality to our commitment. Ben, nestled in my arms, was washed by my tears of despair, and for a moment it seemed my life scheduler had make a mistake. But Bob was in perfect control. With a gentle smile in his eyes, he took my hand and said, "Worry about nothing." I followed him aboard.

This time *Kalmia* had sunk in eleven feet of water, leaving half of her deckhouse exposed to the surging waves of the lashing storm. Once again, the same round table had thrashed about like a trapped fish, battering to smithereens the paneled partition between the galley

and saloon. And worse: *Kalmia* had sunk next to a sewer discharge. Even though Frank had pumped her dry, left in the bilge was a stagnant pool of raw sewage. The mattresses were sewage-soaked, and the previously intact drawers belonging to the built-in mahogany bureau in our stateroom were lying in the muck in pieces like discarded lumber. Trying to fight off hysteria, I became slowly hypnotized by the sight of Bob picking up the pieces of the bureau drawers, taping them together, and sliding them in place while whistling "We Shall Overcome." I became captivated once more by his infectious "anything is possible" attitude, and I knew that we would begin again to turn *Kalmia* into our home. At least we had *Azulykit*, restored and waiting to be hauled on *Kalmia*'s davits.

And if you were wondering about the head, take a look above.

Frank owned a houseboat and offered to let us live on it for the six weeks it would take to get *Kalmia*'s galley and head functioning and staterooms clean enough to sleep in. His houseboat was tied up to an old barge whose surface was rotted and, we agreed, ideal for growing a lawn. Bathed by the white light of a full moon we sowed

the seeds. Within a week the barge was carpeted with sweet-smelling fresh green grass—a perfect antidote for the endless hours of digging, scraping, and hauling 18 inches of foul sewage out of *Kalmia*'s 83 feet of bilge.

The cosmetic injuries suffered from this sinking were most severe in *Kalmia*'s deckhouse.

The paneled wall between the galley and saloon was so splintered it seemed only worth saving for patterns, except the wood was Santo Domingo mahogany and impossible to find in lumberyards. But Bob would not compromise. "Be patient," he said. Meanwhile, there was plenty of other work to do.

[After the crew's quarters were cleaned, Bob brought his tools aboard and built a workbench. His first job was the 11 x 14-foot engine room. For me, that space was a bleak and ominous creature left forgotten. The two 671 GM diesel engines were buried under discarded electric bric-a-brac in a state of confusion and decay. A maze of fuse boxes dangled from the bulkhead, and the spaghetti-like jumble of wires gave no indication what they were or where they belonged. The floor was a chaotic mess of tipped-over wooden boxes with rusty brackets, plumbing fittings, bits of pipe, bolts, nuts, and chain spilling out of them. Then there were the generator, steering cables and shafts, a heating system, water and fuel tanks, and miles of BX cable, badly corroded and seemingly leading everywhere.

Bob loved to tinker with engines, but this, it seemed, was not to be a love affair. Day after day Bob lugged some part of our massive, ominous engines to Frank's machine shop, and his greasy return was often ripe with frustration. "Sail instead?" I asked, a tease he did not take kindly. I stayed out of his way, spending my time on sunny days working on the exterior woodwork. Silver paint on the teak deckhouse, cabin trunk, and hatches was deeply embedded in the open grain of the wood. Removing it required elbow grease, a sharp navy scraper to shave off the silver paint, followed by sheets and sheets of sandpaper in preparation for six coats of rubbed-down varnish.

Cloudy days were reserved for bunging the decks that after so many years of sanding could only hold bungs a quarter-inch thick. And there were always the elusive leaks to locate and caulk, especially the one over our bunk.

The summer sun had brought gold to my hair and a deep tan to my limbs, prompting coarse catcalls from the crews of the nearby pogy boats, followed by, "When you're done, I have plenty of work on my boat." Anger would drive me into the deckhouse, out of sight, except now the flaking paint and the mahogany paneling would stare at me asking for attention. And then there were the endless trips to the laundromat and baths in the galley sink. Ben, now eight months old, was learning to crawl. His pants, shirt, face, hands, and toes became a magnet for invisible grease, necessitating a clean shirt, clean pants, and a bath at least five times a day.

As we scraped back layers of misuse and misfortune, *Kalmia*'s original elegance was revealed and we became hypnotized by the romance. What fools we were to have thought that we would be satisfied to only think of *Kalmia* as a floating house. I knew I was trapped when I found myself scraping and sanding the guardrails in preparation for six coats of varnish when three coats of paint would be sufficient. *Kalmia* had stolen our hearts, and the restoration of her 1909 elegance had become a commitment. But the scowls and chuckles from passersby were not optimistic and there were times when we wondered why we bothered, or if we'd ever finish.

Thanks to a feline, we were brought back into focus. Early one morning we were awakened by a piercing scream. Scrambling on deck and shielding our eyes from the bright dawn sun, we located the source. A kitten had fallen in the water, and its mother, in a futile effort, was trying to get down the piling to rescue it. Bob jumped into *Azulykit*, untied her from *Kalmia*'s stern, paddled over, and retrieved the drowning kitten. Back onboard, we dried and soothed the scared little kitten. Within the hour, the mother had found us. She came aboard, prowled about, checked us out, sniffed her kitten, and left.

We scooped up the kitten and followed her to a wharf building where her remaining litter of six was stashed. Returning the kitten to its siblings, we left to go about our business. Then, after a much-needed dinner out, we returned to discover that Mrs. Cat and her seven kittens were happily ensconced in *Kalmia*'s saloon. One by one she had carried them down the dock, across the gangplank, and into the saloon. A formidable job! We considered this an honor and, with our self-esteem preened, we agreed that one of her kittens should be brought up in what their mother had decided was a palace. We returned the other six to the wharf building, keeping one, which we named it Putt-putt as a reminder that progress was slow but sure.

❖

Kalmia's berth was next to Newport's Long Wharf, on a street full of bars frequented by sailors. Brawls would start in early afternoon and often lasted until well after midnight. Twice *Azulykit* was "borrowed" by drunken sailors, and the last time it took us three frantic days to find her. So when we were offered free dockage at Williams and Manchester's Boatyard, we were anxious to move. The engines were barely back together, but enough (we prayed) to make the half-mile trip south from Long Wharf.

Williams and Manchester was a different type of boatyard. For years it had been a privileged home for the *America*'s Cup defenders and the dowager yachts that hovered around them like pilot fish. That era gone, the boatyard opened its pier to the public, and a restaurant was built by the water's edge to extend its business to accommodate a new kind of yachtsman, referred to as "armchair sailors." Our new berth found us located directly in front of the restaurant, its many windows stealing our privacy. We had become a ploy to attract more diners, including the after-dinner strollers who often leaned over our rail to peer in the windows or who came aboard without asking. As a classic boat, *Kalmia* was a conversation piece, but as a house she made us prisoners to our commitment.

But living there did have advantages. Some of the dockside spectators remembered *Kalmia* in her days of glory cruising the southern New England waters. The most astonishing tale came from one individual who told us that our 6-71 diesels that had replaced her original gasoline engines in the 1940s, had themselves been retrieved from a sunken wreck off Block Island. This meant that these engines Bob had been so diligently working on had been sunk a total of three times!

"Breaks them in," Bob said.

We were given gifts. One was a "pudding boom" from an old yachtsman. Its purpose was to protect the tender as it hung from the davits. In our case, *Azulykit* would have that pleasure. And from another came an ancient "patent log" for determining speed and distance traveled.

And then there was the day I was painting the canvas deck over the deckhouse when I heard a gentle voice call, "Is anybody home?" Looking down, I saw a tiny woman, her white hair buffeted by the wind was dancing about like fair-weather clouds. She smiled up at me invitingly. I jumped down, joined her on the dock, and shook her delicate hand.

"I wanted to tell you that you and your husband are doing a wonderful job. " she said. "My deceased husband and I salvaged and lived on an old boat much like yours, and I know the amount of work involved."

Then, glowing like a grandmother, she launched into an amazing proposal. "I would like to help," she said. "I sew." If I bought the canvas, she offered to make the missing wind curtains (canvas attached between the rails and the deck.) It was my turn to glow. I felt like a happy grandchild and looked at her with wondrous thanks.

Each of these gifts was very special, but nothing as special as the day I was given a vacuum cleaner, a treasure we could put to immediate use.

Kalmia was becoming everybody's project, perceived now as a heritage worth preserving.

When *Kalmia* was launched in 1909, she was registered and documented, her certificate maintained by successive owners until 1951. Now that we were the owners, we definitely wanted to certify that she was still in existence. There were many advantages for documentation: size, tonnage, chain of title, ease of customs, preferred mortgages, and so on. For Bob, it would make her official again, and most important, she would not have to wear Coast Guard numbers on her hull.

Kalmia, 1919

We visited the U.S. Custom House in New Bedford, Massachusetts. Built in 1834, it is the oldest continuously operated customhouse in the nation. Sitting high on a hill, the building had been visible from whaling ships before the shades of urban growth had been drawn. Greek Revival in design, it was two stories of white granite. As we walked up the granite steps and under the portico held up by fluted granite columns, I thought about the whaling masters, and perhaps Herman Melville himself, who had walked up these very same steps more than a hundred years ago to register their ships. Inside, we found a sign "U.S. Customs," and a poster of Uncle Sam, his figure pointing up instead of at us. At the top of the stairs was a door with peeling layers of yellowed varnish, but not around the area behind the knob, well-worn from years of shipowners opening and closing it. Inside, a Coast Guard officer explained that in order to bring *Kalmia*'s documentation up to date, we would have to provide all the names of her previous owners. Between the customhouse records and *Lloyd's Register of American Yachts*, we found that in 1909, the year of her launching, she was owned by Hobart Parks of New York, an heir to a grocery fortune. That same year Parks sold *Kalmia* to Oliver Grinnell who sold the boat to Harry Anderson in 1919.

The following year Anderson sold *Kalmia* to Frederick Vanderbilt, the builder of Rough Point, as his mansion in Newport was named, and later the home of Doris Duke. Vanderbilt sold the boat to M. S. Bentham in 1925. Bentham sold her to John Rhodes of New Bedford. Rhodes owned *Kalmia* for eleven years and then sold her to John Duff in 1938 (above) who replaced her gasoline engines with the

Kalmia, 1963

two GM 6-71 diesels. Duff sold *Kalmia* to the Boston Coast Guard in 1951, at which time her chain of documentation ended. The next owner was Robert B. Law, a trucker from Providence who used *Kalmia* as a weekend family retreat and I suspect was the culprit that painted the teak saloon silver, painted the swordfish on the stack, and layered the deck in racing-red paint. Law owned *Kalmia* until Tiger purchased her after she sank 1963.

We were amazed to discover that during all those years of different owners her name had never been changed.

Two months later, with all her owners found, *Kalmia* was again documented, with the privilege of flying an ensign and be entered in the *Lloyd's Register of American Yachts*.

During the search for her past owners, we found her original builder's plans and discovered that the shelter over the bridge, and the teak settee at the forward end of her deckhouse, were not original. Committed to her 1909 restoration, we removed them. Sixty years later, the settee sits comfortably under my studio window in Westport, a constant reminder of *Kalmia*.

By the following winter Bob had installed a new furnace and repaired the heating system. New windows had been installed in the saloon, the delinquent table repaired, curtains hung, and new cushions graced the settees. The saloon, galley, and our stateroom were clean and usable.

As complement to her décor, or fear of cold damp days, we installed a wood-burning stove in the salon—its finishing touch a copper smokestack.

Bob continued to scrape and paint, while coping with a tottering son who was determined to be a ship's captain.

The wind curtains that the woman had promised were hung and served an even greater function as child retainer after we added an inner, expandable fence for extra precaution against Ben falling overboard.

We had yet to find the Santo Domingo mahogany for the saloon's interior repair. The work

on the port side of the deckhouse had barely begun, another baby was due in December, and the heating system was plugged with mud. We decided to take our 83-foot house south to look for warm working weather. Destination: Nassau, Bahamas.

In preparation for the Nassau trip, we had the yard haul her out, paint her topsides, her bottom, and align her propeller shafts to their engines. With *Kalmia* back in the water, we took a trial spin around the harbor. Although it was impossible to talk when the engines were running, they proved ready. Her performance at sea still remained an unknown. *Kalmia* was designed for a crew of three, plus a captain and engineer. It would be a lot of boat for two people to handle, but I felt confident in our abilities and knew that Bob, as a marine architect, had a good understanding of her cruising capabilities.

Photographs: Personal collection.

Nassau

Again, the sunrise brought a perfect day for the beginning of a new adventure. Her engines purring, *Kalmia* was as ready as were we. We hauled in our lines and gently pulled away from our slip. Ben and I joined Bob on the bridge and as he pointed *Kalmia*'s bow towards the southern sky, yesterday's clouds reflected the promising rays of a new September day. Pulling my sweater around my shoulders, I waved good-by to Newport and two years of good friends.

By the time we reached Long Island Sound, our seagoing responsibilities had become established—Bob as helmsman, navigator, mechanic, and I as a crew of three. The following day we reached New York City and maneuvered down the East River, feeling extremely glamorous. In return, our 1900 elegance was greeted by saluting horns. A lump rose in my throat and a shiver went down my spine. I looked over at Bob, and we shared a gratifying smile. The New Yorkers could only see the starboard side—our best side, with six coats of varnish on the brightwork. The port side still looked like an underwater aquarium.

Entering New York Bay, we were enveloped by fog. Our showtime over and with no desire to collide with an oil barge, we aimed for the nearest haven, the Brooklyn Boatyard. I've always wondered if *Kalmia* had anything to do with our decision. The boatyard was a treasure chest of yacht artifacts usable for her restoration. For years it had been a marine wrecking yard, breaking up old yachts, steamboats, and ships such as those from the Fall River Line. Stored in a shed was an astonishing collection of parts and pieces: elegant cabin doors, hatches, settees, cupboards, paneling, brass hardware, lights and lanterns, and even the Santo Domingo mahogany Bob had been patiently waiting for. With the days of big wooden ships gone, the yard was being converted into a marina and the storage shed slated

for demolition. Its contents were up for grabs, and like gluttons, we had filled the forward end of *Kalmia* by the end of the day—granted, more than we would ever need, but then one never knew.

Three days later, the weather cleared and we headed for the Atlantic Ocean bordering the New Jersey coast. This stretch of coastline is traditionally known for its rough water and would be the first genuine sea trial for *Kalmia* and her crew.

The sea was calm as we started down the coast, but within an hour the gentle easterly breezes shifted to strong westerly winds, and an inky grim sky. Then, as the horizon disappeared, a squall descended. Bob, alone on the bridge, lashed himself to the binnacle, and I secured all loose objects in the deckhouse. Suddenly the seas began to smash against the windows and *Kalmia* bucked about as if awakening to a forgotten rhythm. Ben was tossed around like a rubber ball until I found my sea legs and grabbed him. I was unable to communicate with Bob, as the bridge was not accessible from the saloon. In the meantime, *Kalmia* was delighted by her first time out in years. She'd lean way, way over, and each time I worried that she might forget to come back. Then, suddenly, wham! up she'd come and repeat the same performance in the opposite direction. I began to trust her, but I knew this kind of action was making steering impossible for Bob. I was afraid to even think about the consequences if he was thrown overboard. I desperately wanted to see if he was okay or even if he was still there, but it was not safe to let go of Ben and I didn't dare take him out onto the deck, as we both would surely get pitched into the sea. Huddling in the corner, we waited. My only distraction was watching the wooden bowl of apples on the table slide back and forth with the rolling. Just when the bowl was about to dump on the floor the roll would reverse and the bowl would slide the other way, just in time. The bowl had found its center of gravity, but had Bob?

Two hours later the seas subsided and *Kalmia* settled down exhausted. Fearfully, I crept outside and found a very soggy husband with a huge smile of relief on his face. I didn't know whether to laugh or cry. "Just ease her when she pitches," he said. A saying he used often now had a potent meaning.

Kalmia was okay, we were okay, and from that moment on I was convinced that Bob was a reincarnated sea captain. Now, when I look back, I realize that Bob was having a blast testing how an 83-foot boat with a narrow beam of 14 feet would perform in a sea.

By evening the comforting lights of Atlantic City came in sight. Again, remembering our New York response, we managed to keep a starboard profile as we entered the harbor. Tying up, we found we were one of many yachts heading south via the ICW (Intracoastal Waterway), none looking as undisciplined as *Kalmia,* caked with salt water. The next morning, the salt washed off, decks swabbed, dishes restacked, and fresh apples in the bowl, we let go our lines and headed for the Delaware River.

Our first bridge of the day was a hand-operated swing bridge. As we approached, we blew the long and short blasts to signal the bridge to open. But the attendant, engrossed with a friend, a cup of coffee, and go-along conversation, was in no hurry to heed us. In the meantime, the current was forcing us down on the bridge. I looked over at Bob. His stubby pipe was clenched between his teeth. He signaled again, then put one engine in reverse, to "back her down" as he'd say, while waiting for the bridge to open. Backing her down was successful but also permanent! Bob, a devilish look on his face, handed me a broken reverse control lever. Relying on our second engine, he decided to maneuver to a nearby dolphin, tie up, and reattach the control lever The situation however, got worse. The steering cable snapped. Now crippled by our machinery we had only one alternative: reverse ourselves onto the beach. As the tide receded, we slowly listed and soon became 83 feet of beached animal, an ominous sight for passing yachts. Every captain looked the other way. Offering help could mean a day lost on their trip south. But then, what else could be expected from yachts with names like *Pearl Necklace, Real Deal,* and *My Wife's Fur Coat?*

You might ask why we didn't radio for help. "Radio? Who needs that?" was Bob's attitude on leaving Newport, an attitude that also meant we had no radar, depth sounder, or loran. Stubborn as he was, he would have refused help even if it had arrived. Of course, in time, he had everything back in working order. The tide rose and we slowly worked our way off the beach by using the anchor, engine, and push-and-pull method. This time the bridge opened. We headed up Delaware Bay, crossed through the Chesapeake and Delaware Canal, entered Chesapeake Bay, and in two more days reached Annapolis, where we planned to rendezvous with Bill Norton and his charter boat *Empress.*

Bill, Frank Norton's brother, chartered out of Newport in the summer and Nassau in the winter. He was salty as they come: crusted cheeks, pleated forehead, and ropy arms that tirelessly lifted a shot of rum belied his tender side. He insisted we travel in tandem. This, he convinced us, would take the strain off the unknown and eliminate further potential mishaps on *Kalmia*'s maiden voyage. We went up creeks, celebrated Ben's second birthday on a sandy beach with his new pail and shovel, and picked pink flowers from the overhanging camellia trees in the Dismal Swamp Canal as we passed through into North Carolina. If we lagged too far behind, Bill would wait. He had many old cronies along the inland waterway to gossip with.

Ben was happy. He and Putt-Putt had become buddies. Putt-Putt retained the wharf instincts he was born with and knew exactly when we were about to come in for the night. Positioned on our bow at strike posture, he would jump the three remaining feet to the dock and disappear. In some mysterious way reserved for cats, he would reappear only moments before we cast off in the morning. For me, though, the job of securing our bow line to a piling presented a problem. With a tummy full with an unborn child, I didn't dare jump the three feet to the dock. Swallowing my pride I made sure my condition was obvious hoping somebody would offer to catch the other end of the line. It never failed.

By the end of October we reached the northern tip of Florida and put in for the night at Fernandina Beach, the gateway to orange juice, including two free ounces. Exhausted, we descended to our fully-restored quarters—two spacious staterooms and a head complete with tub. After months of work, the sheen on the white painted paneling contrasted stunningly with the newly varnished mahogany trim. All the hours of cleaning, sanding, and painting had been worth it. Our quarters were as luxurious as a cabin on the *Queen Mary*. I fell into bed content. Sleep came instantly—but also morning and time to get underway again. I rubbed my eyes, opened them, and blinked. The white painted walls were covered with large brown splotches as if ink had been thrown at them. Reflections I thought, and settled in for a last snooze. But just to be sure I reached up with a shaking finger and rubbed at a spot. The brown splotches didn't budge.

"Oh, my God." I screamed.

Bob's eyes popped open and I pointed at the splotches.

"Now you've done it!" he mischievously said.

"Not funny," I replied, punching my elbow in to his side.

Stunned and confused we got out of bed, slid open the hatch, and looked about for the cause. The scene was unfathomable. Brown splotches covered the village houses, our white topsides, and our polished brass had turned a deathly green color. Frantic, I yelled to the nearest person, "What's happened?"

"It's the sulfur from the pulp mills. It settles on quiet nights. It will fade" he said. "Otherwise use Clorox."

Fade! How long would that take? Since I couldn't reach the topsides to clean, I attacked what had been our pristine stateroom.

Clorox straight up did the job. By bedtime the cabin was clean, as were my fingers, having been bleached a deadly white. By the time we reached Miami, the stains on the topsides had faded, but only elbow grease had put back the shine on the brass.

Miami was the last stop before crossing the Gulf Stream: open water that has a notorious reputation for a strong currant, fierce north winds, and 8- to 10-foot waves that hug each other so close that the seas become untenable. While waiting for a south to southwest wind, ideal for the eight-hour crossing, we laid over at Jones Boat-yard four miles up the Miami River. This gave Bob a chance to find and replace other decayed parts and pieces connected to the engines, Ben to regain land-legs, and Putt-Putt to establish a serious romance. And, as if on an endless portage, I kept sanding, varnishing, and growing larger with child. Finally, after three weeks of gluttonous mosquitoes and the deafening sounds of jet takeoffs, Bill announced, "The weather's right. It's now or never." Our experience learned from the New Jersey Coast had taught us the full meaning of the term "shipshape," and this time we were ready.

We took our position behind the *Empress* and headed southeast for the eighteen hours it would take to get to Nassau. *Kalmia* was in her element and acted with gentle restraint as we crossed the Gulf Stream. As we got closer to Nassau, the cold gray Atlantic changed to a spectrum of beautiful turquoise shades.

"From here on, navigation is strictly by the color of the water," Bill said. After a few brushes with the sea floor we found the right

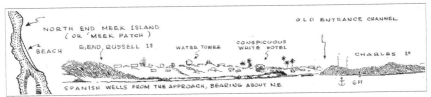

NORTH END MEEK ISLAND
(OR 'MEEK PATCH)
OLD ENTRANCE CHANNEL
BEACH   E,END, RUSSELL I?   WATER TOWER   CONSPICUOUS WHITE HOTEL   CHARLES I?
SPANISH WELLS FROM THE APPROACH, BEARING ABOUT N.E.   6 FT

Typical chart for navigating in the Bahamas

color for *Kalmia*'s 4-foot draft and followed it like a roadmap.

In 1963 the nautical charts had only a few soundings, and if one needed to know where one was, it meant comparing the humps, hollows, and rooftops of an island's landmass to a hand-drawn profile sketched in a directory. What you saw is where you were.

Three weeks after reaching Nassau, our daughter Sarah was born. The next day Bob and I proudly carried her home to Ben, Putt-Putt, and *Kalmia*.

While resting in Nassau, Bob became fascinated by the fishing boats known as Bahamian smacks. Their huge, lopping sails of multi-

colored patchwork gracefully spilling into the water was a delight to see. But it was their V-shaped squat hulls, fine entries, graceful sheers, low freeboard, and the distinctive heart-shaped transoms unique to these boats that immediately captured Bob's heart. He took many photographs as he watched them coming and going in Nassau's harbor. Inspired by what he was seeing, he began to draw a set of lines. He wasn't planning to design a smack boat but wanted to capture on paper the spirit of their shape. Before Bob was satisfied he had built two models to see clearly what he had been seeing in his head. The first model was 4 inches long and featured a lapstrake hull, a mast, rigging, thwarts, frames, centerboard, rudder, tiller, and all the fittings in miniature scale. The second model was 12 inches long and was only the hull, each strake glued on piece-by-piece, to help him determine the construction. Satisfied with his plans, Bob named the dinghy design Bembo after our son Ben.

Bill Page, a yacht broker and sailor who lived in Camden, Maine, wanted a dinghy. He asked his good friend Bob, if he had plans for

Bembo
LOA: 11′0″; Beam: 4′9 ¾″

one. When Bob showed him the plans of the Bembo, Bill said, "That's it!" and Bill went ahead and built the boat, which he named *Nellie*.

"*Nellie*," Bill later wrote, "Is the one boat in which I would change absolutely nothing and would not part with her for any price. Bob did an outstanding job when designing her."

Bob's ability to understand shape is an art that few people achieve, and this art is what guided him all his life.

Waiting for Sarah to get a bit older before motoring on, we spent time exploring the town and nearby Paradise Island. In 1965, Nassau

was still an English colony and had yet to be abused by developers. With Ben, Sarah, and a picnic, we often rowed *Azulykit* across the harbor to Paradise Island. The entrance, through an emerald green, vine-entwined canal, led into an abandoned lagoon that quivered with unbelievable beauty and a mysterious past. The lagoon, fed by the ocean through a cut through the island, was surrounded by walls of white coral encrusted with the shades of the sea. Crumbling marble statuaries; a lush, overgrown tropical garden; birds chattering in the tropical trees; and the pink shells of Angel Wings glowing like a sunset made it seem as if nymphs had turned the surroundings into a fairytale. I stripped and plunged into the crystal clear water.

It's gone now, replaced by a casino, a bridge for tour buses; the smack boats replaced by cruise ships; dazzling beauty assaulted by developers.

When Sarah was six weeks old we headed for Highborn Cay, an island a few hours east of Nassau. Bill Norton, friendly with the people who managed the island's aloe plantation, had arranged for us to have a free winter berth. But it wasn't exactly free! In exchange for wharfage, we were occasionally asked to act as a freight boat. This

meant a trip to Nassau to purchase the dynamite used for clearing the forest for growing aloe plants. Although the dynamite was carefully stowed, each white-capped wave initiated panic.

Other than the occasional dynamite blasting, the island was snug and peaceful, ideal for work and play. The boat basin was tucked under the island's hilly backbone and next to a white sandy beach with smooth turquoise water. It was a paradise for Ben and Sarah.

Beachcombing on the north end of the island brought a great discovery when Bob's keen eyes spotted a large piece of driftwood. He identified it as Santo Domingo mahogany and lugged it back to *Kalmia*. Taking it below to his "workshop," he grinned and announced a surprise was on its way. A few days later, returning from the beach with the children, I stepped into the galley to discover that the driftwood had been transformed into an exquisite newel post, now installed at the top of the companionway ladder. With this finishing touch the deckhouse was complete.

But not *Kalmia*'s topsides. The paint kept peeling like a snake shedding its skin. After being sunk for six months, her wooden hull was saturated with salt, which forced the paint off. I wondered if latex house paint would hold better than the marine oil-based paint I'd been using. I decided to try latex, but when I told Bob he shook his head in disgust. Too bad, I told him. Tired of constantly scraping, patching, and painting I had nothing to lose. It worked, but of course

Bob would never admit that latex paint, instead of good, old-fashioned boat paint actually solved the problem.

Photographs: Personal collection.
Nellie was featured in *WoodenBoat* magazine No. 1.

Heading Home

By late spring of 1966 we had accomplished the work we had set out to do. *Kalmia*'s topsides and decks were immaculate, and with the six coats of varnish on the deckhouse, cabin trunk, hatches, and rails, her brightwork glowed. It was time to head home.

As a going-away present, our Highborn Cay friends presented us with a marine radio. They'd decided that the boat was okay to be vintage but we were not! Although by now we knew what to expect or not to expect from *Kalmia,* having a marine radio felt more secure.

We pulled in our lines and headed out. As usual, our travels were ruled by curiosity. Instead of heading west towards Nassau, Florida, and the Intracoastal Waterway, we went northeast to Eleuthera. We spent a night in Cupids Cay—now named Governors Harbor—exploring and photographing the ancient abandoned buildings. It was fortunate for Bob that the forward end of *Kalmia* was already filled with a collection of wood we'd scavenged from the Brooklyn Marina. Otherwise I would have rescued some pieces of paneling from the interior of the Governor's Mansion to take home and add them to my collection of old building parts.

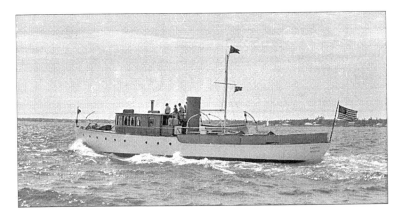

From there we headed north following the west shore of Eleuthera, then hooked around to the east near St. George's Cay. Bob had been told there was a narrow, shallow passage between St. George's Cay and Russell's Island—along with the advice, "Don't try it." Regardless, we headed for the passage knowing that with *Kalmia*'s shallow draft, skinny beam, and her willingness to explore, we could make it through. Slowly navigating the shallow turquoise water, we must have looked like a city moving in. Within twenty minutes a waving crowd of natives lined the shore, cheering and waving us ahead to a tiny dock. Clearly they wanted us to stop. Was this a friendly gesture or abduction? Escape could only be one knot of speed at the most. We pulled in anyway and were greeted by huge smiles and a bag of conchs as a gift. It was the first time they had seen a boat this big pass through the cut.

After a tour of our boat, and some navigating advice from our new friends, we successfully reached the other side of the cut, the Straits of Florida, and our route to Fort Lauderdale. Other than a loose propeller with the inevitable haul-out, *Kalmia*'s engines and attached parts purred up the waterway.

But Bob had one last place that he wanted to test: to see how well *Kalmia* could navigate the New Jersey ICW. We were long, we were narrow, and we only drew 4 feet, and again, we were advised not to try it; the route was very narrow with tight bends, exactly the reason Bob had to find out how well *Kalmia*'s shape, size, and draft could navigate the many sinuous bends. At Manasquan, New Jersey, Bob poked *Kalmia*'s nose into the Waterway. But the one thing that *Kalmia* wasn't was a snake. At each bend this meant pushing out her stern then racing to the bow to push her bow out and then reversing the operation at the next opposite bend. An hour later, reaching open water, *Kalmia*'s topsides were cleaned of the ICW's grassy residue, and she looked as if she had never been in one of those places that a boat her size should never go.

Reaching Long Island Sound, we made a side trip before Newport and home. While in the Bahamas we had met Jack Kochiss, another "old-boat nut," who told us about a derelict 1870s Whitehall that he had stowed away in his backyard in Bridgeport, Connecticut. It was ours for the taking.

Bob, never turning down an old-boat offer, turned north from Long Island Sound and into the harbor at Bridgeport. Picked up by Jack, we were driven to his house. The boat, stored outside for years, was lying upside-down in his woods. When we picked her up to turn her over, she bent in the middle as if she were a mattress. But Bob, a great believer that anything can be restored, took a long look at her.

"The parts that are almost gone," he said, "are her oak sheer planks; the keel is not much good; the clamps are not much good; and her frames are not much to write home about, but it seems to me that she has a shape and her planking isn't all that bad." Because of some newer planks, Bob felt that at some point she had been hit by something. But regardless, she was in good enough shape to give an inkling of what she had been. The look on his face told me there was something important about her.

Back at the dock we loaded her aboard *Kalmia,* and now, in the bright sunlight, Bob noticed that the name *T. Donoghue,* was stamped into her backrest. With *Donoghue* secured on deck we headed for Newport, timing our arrival to coincide with the start of the 1966 Newport-to-Bermuda Race. Placing *Kalmia* in the midst of the huge spectator fleet, she was instantly remembered as that derelict towed into Newport three years previously. We were welcomed home with cheers, whistles, and backslapping as we proudly showed her off— this time from every angle, her renaissance complete.

Photographs: Personal collection.

Warren

Tied up again in Newport, we knew we needed a land base of our own, away from commercial wharfage with its rules and regulations, and from the spectators who sucked away our privacy. Bob heard about an old oyster building built on a wharf in Warren, Rhode Island, that was for sale.

The wharf and pilings were secure enough to tie *Kalmia* to. The building was three stories high, with three large first-floor rooms, one of them ideal for restoring boats, another I could use for repairing old house woodwork, and the other a safe place for Ben and Sarah to play. On the west side was a small lean-to that was perfect for Bob's office. The second floor had a two-bedroom rentable apartment and there was a full attic. The place even had enough land on the east end for a kitchen garden. We bought it.

Now that Bob had a good-sized space in which to design, restore, and build boats, he moved his tools in. Bob loved tools. Whatever he

did, how he did it was just as important as getting it done. A tool for him was an extension of his hands, with the resulting work flowing directly from his mind. Everything was hand-planed, hand-cut, hand-drilled. The only tool that used electricity was a huge cast-iron bandsaw that was older than Bob by fifty years. Bob's tools were so precious to him that you could feel his eyes on your back if you were using one, and once when I made the mistake of setting a plane down on its sole—well, you can imagine.

Next, he organized his office: shelves for his books; filing cabinets for his collection of photographs, research, and letters; a drafting table; and a rug on the floor to keep his feet warm. When designing, Bob used a ruling pen: a stick with a nib on the end. He had infinite patience; one nib full of ink didn't last very long before he would have to dip again into the ink. After the pen was filled, he'd jerk it a few times towards the floor to get the amount of ink just right, and that's how the new rug under his feet slowly changed to oriental.

Many people were in need of Bob's skills and it wasn't long before boats were lined up in the water next to our shop.

Our commitment to stay here would mean *Kalmia*'s restored exterior would be subjected to harsh winter weather. We shivered when looking at *Kalmia*—a beautiful piece of furniture being attacked by frigid winter wind and snow with ice crashing against her coppered waterline. This kept Bob awake with worry.

Summer versus winter

When all our nine children were with us—our two, my five, and Bob's two sons Stephen and Jeremy from his first marriage (who visited from England), life aboard was chaotic. They loved it, of course, but dealing with nine children surrounded by water instead of land meant life jackets and a constant head count.

And in the winter it was treacherous carrying one child and leading the other across slippery decks to reach their staterooms below, especially when finding the hatch frozen closed. We had become slaves to the yacht we had recreated, and it soon became obvious that we needed to think how *Kalmia* would fit our future.

After two more winters, we put *Kalmia* up for sale. Bob was suspicious of every potential buyer, particularly if the woman was wearing high-heeled shoes. When one couple was discussing how to modernize *Kalmia*'s interior he quickly ushered them down the gangplank. After six potential buyers had been "gangplanked," David Montgomery and his wife appeared. They loved the boat for just what it was, and in 1967 became her new owners. With *Kalmia* gone, we moved into the apartment above the shop that we had previously rented out. Visiting the Montgomerys a year later, we were delighted to see that nothing had changed. The varnish glowed, the same sage green curtains hung in the saloon, and there were fresh apples on the table.

Photographs: Personal collection.

Wherries and Whitehalls

For the next year or so *Donoghue* sat in the corner of the Warren shop where I'd often see Bob staring at her. When visitors came by, their usual comment was, "God, Baker, what did you save that thing for?!" Tired of hearing negative remarks, Bob decided to restore her. As usual, he walked around the boat with his hands behind his back, occasionally stopping to strike a match with his fingernail, light his pipe, and then continue to poke and prod. He'd tie little things here and there, pulled and pushed, and after a while her plank lines started to come together and with more poking and prodding he was able to get her into some semblance of order. "So what the hell," he announced, "let's measure her."

Now, with a set of lines to go by, he built outside molds and very, very gently started to strip her out. But before placing her in the molds, Bob put her in the river, leaving her to sink for the better part of a week so she could soak up and get a little more limber. When she was as pliable as seaweed, he got everybody he could find to help lift her out and then gently set her into the molds. She fit.

He then fastened her into the molds with little tabs screwed through her hull to hold her solidly. Next, he removed the keel and the stem. Slowly, after Bob replaced the sternpost and a piece of the transom, her shape began to look like what it once was. Next, Bob replaced the entire keel. After checking all the bevels and ensuring

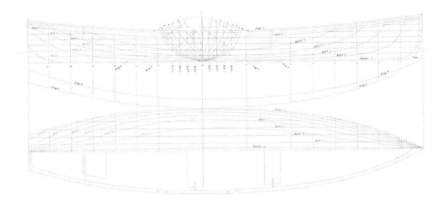

Donoghue
LOA: 17'11³/8"; Beam: 3'9³/8"
Measured and drawn by RHB

that everything was coming along nicely, he replaced the stem, the sheer planks, and all her frames (except for one pair that could be reused) along with two thwarts and some planking. Bob commented, "As the new wood was going into her I could imagine her saying, "Oh boy, this is the best thing that has happened to me in years."

Bob could see that at one point she had been hit—"cut right down the middle." He felt that whoever had replaced those planks had done quite a creditable job, "All butt, not a lap in the lot, but nicely done," he said. "Those butts are neat because they show part of her history. They show that somebody had fixed her, somebody cared, somebody liked her enough to rebuild her once and then we came along and I figured what the hell, let's rebuild her again."

Bob also felt that, amazingly, both *Azulykit* and *Donoghue* were built in George Kneiss's shop in Clinton, Connecticut The details of construction and the decorative bead cut along the length of the sheer plank are similar to several yawlboats attributed to Kneiss and also similar to more extreme boats such as *Donoghue*, built in Clinton in the 1870s—the same period that Kneiss had his shop there.

By comparing *Donoghue*'s and *Azulykit*'s plans, it was obvious that their construction was the same except *Donoghue*'s was lighter and finer in all her details and could not possibly have handled freight. Bob determined that even though *Donoghue* was Whitehall-built, she was actually a wherry—an English word that simply delineates her light framing as a pleasure boat, a gentleman's rowing boat.

Bob was temporarily stumped when he couldn't find an impression or the screw holes where *Donoghue*'s oarlocks had been. He did notice four places where two square cuts had been chiseled into her gunwales where something had been inserted. He remembered seeing a picture somewhere of a patented oarlock that had two tabs. He started to look in the crusty old catalogs we had found and saved from Brock's shop and found a full-size etching of an outrigger oarlock, complete with measurements, and tabs that exactly matched the size of the cuts on *Donoghue*'s gunwale. From a piece of basswood he whittled out the three parts needed for an outrigger oarlock, took the patterns to a foundry, and had two pairs cast in bronze. They worked beautifully; and with the outriggers, our oars could be longer, which made for smoother rowing.

Bob thought that her colors were interesting. "Her interior was Band-Aid pink and the color I should have used, explaining that the pink paint was made from a combination of red lead and blue lead called laphaig. The Band-Aid pink came from diluting the red with this laphaig. Instead, he chose French gray but felt he should have stuck with the pink.

"It's always all about history," Bob remarked.

As proud owners of *Donoghue*, we decided to show her off at the 1969 Rowing Workshop at Mystic Seaport. Sleek and beautiful with a delicate wine glass transom, she couldn't help but attract John Gardner's attention, who was then the Museum's associate curator of small craft, a teacher, and an author of books about boatbuilding. Gardner wandered over, walked around *Donoghue* a few times, then declared, "Nice Whitehall."

Not one to be shy when it comes to talking boats, Bob bit down on his pipe and replied, "Too light and fine for a Whitehall. She's a wherry, a gentleman's pulling boat. "

"No," John said, "she is Whitehall-built and therefore a Whitehall." And that was the beginning of, shall we say, a lively discussion until fortunately a downpour intervened.

Driving home at the end of that day, I asked Bob to explain to me the details that identified a Whitehall or a wherry. Because we owned *Azulykit*, I knew that a Whitehall had a wineglass-shaped transom, two rowing stations, and used a spritsail rig when sailed. And I knew that the rudder was controlled by an attached yoke and lines instead of a tiller. I could see that the construction was carvel-planked with white cedar, with oak sheer planks that overlapped the second or "binding" plank. "But if you ever get into a discussion about what is and what isn't a Whitehall, that's not enough," Bob said. And then explained:

The steam-bent oak frames are riveted square to the centerline of the boat and attached across the oak keel with a natural crook floor timber. The top of the frames are covered by an oak inwale, the inner edge of which has a decorative bead, as do the natural crook quarter knees and breast hook. The sternpost is beaded on both edges. The stern seats are U-shaped and both these and the thwarts are beaded on their edges, as is the seat riser. The thwart knees are natural crooks. The transom has a graceful, reverse S-curve often referred to as wineglass in shape, a characteristic that is Whitehall but not without the other components. Forward of the transom is a removable backrest where the name of the boat was carved or painted.

Yes, I had forgotten about the backrest, which both our Whitehall and wherry have, but I did wonder how he could keep this all straight in his head and promised myself to never get into an argument like he had with John Gardner.

Bob felt that a Whitehall was a descendent of the yawlboat like the ones we found in Brock's shop in Inverness: an open workboat, long and narrow, with a wineglass transom, used as a ship's tender. "The shape is not dissimilar," he said. Bob told me that, historically, the name Whitehall was given to open rowing craft built in the boat shops on Whitehall Street in New York City as early as 1820. Those were the days when the New York Harbor was filled with hundreds of sailing ships loading and unloading their wares into or out of Whitehalls.

There are those who have a Whitehall and those that give the term Whitehall to any boat with a wineglass stern, and a whole bunch that look like a Whitehall but were not thought to be when built. If you think you know what a Whitehall is, that feeling could leave you completely confused.

After arriving home, I went to the edge of our wharf, sat down, and tried to sort through the confusion of what is and what isn't. Looking through the evening's mist, I heard the soft swish of oars as a sleek 15-foot pulling boat cut through the inky water like a knife and, as quickly, disappeared leaving an image of a wineglass transom. Was it a Whitehall?

Both *Donoghue* and *Azulykit* are now in Mystic Seaport Museum's watercraft collection.

Photographs: Personal collection.

Sandbaggers

It is not unusual to hear the name sandbagger and think gambling. But not for Bob. He knew that a sandbagger was a boat originally designed for working the oyster beds. Small and light, often referred to as a skimming dish, a sandbagger was ideal for sailing in shoal waters, for mooring on mud flats, and for fishing in areas too distant to reach by rowing. In the 1860s and '70s, boat racing was still in its infancy. Long Island Sound looked very different a century ago. Now we're used to seeing it dotted with the sails of pleasure boats. But back then, we would have seen working craft: schooners and square-riggers carrying cargo, and small fishing boats. Pleasure boating was largely the sport of the very wealthy, with large yachts manned by professional captains and crews. But in that pre-automobile era, every waterfront town and farm had small, wide, shoal-draft catboats and sloops as a regular means of getting about. And out of these, starting around 1800 in the New York area, came the sandbagger.

The sandbagger has a plumb stem and stern, a beam about 40 percent of its length, flaring topsides, an oval, open cockpit, a jib-and-mainsail rig, and sometimes two mast steps so it could be sailed either as a sloop or a cat. A sandbagger had both a working rig and a much larger rig for racing. The racing rigs were extravagant, with a bowsprit nearly as long as the hull, an enormous jib, and a long boomkin for sheeting the huge mainsail. The final racing sandbaggers had a "sparred" length easily twice that of the hull itself. There was no limitation on sail area, and shifting ballast (sandbags filled with gravel), moved by an active, agile crew on each tack made it possible to carry these huge rigs.

Over the years Bob had studied models, looked at old photographs, examined three surviving sandbaggers, and felt not all of them were out-and-out racing machines. He knew that the same type was also used as a workboat or watch boat. Because of their speed, watch boats were used to protect the oyster beds from poachers.

In 1966 an opportunity for deeper research appeared when Gordon Douglas, of Westbury, Connecticut, approached Bob. Douglas, who was actively involved in the restoration of Newport's early houses, was also interested in saving old boats. He had heard that a sandbagger named *Shadow* was for sale and wanted Bob to take a look. "I'm not specifically looking for a sandbagger to buy," he told Bob, "but I am interested in trying to save old boats, since their historic significance is not yet generally appreciated."

Shadow, owned by Dr. William Teuscher, was stored in a shed in Westport, Connecticut. After a complete survey, Bob told Douglas that *Shadow* was a rare and special find and certainly worthy of purchase and restoration. "She is important and a wonderful old boat," Bob told him.

In December of 1966, *Shadow* was delivered to our shop in Warren. Sitting in our yard, her sleek profile was beautiful to look at and now Bob took time to poke and prod while explaining to me what he had found so I could take notes as follows:

> *Dr. Teuscher added a shoe to her keel to stiffen the hull.*
> *He put in a new outer stem with a little flare at the top, but this does not belong to the original boat.*
> *The kingplank will have to be removed, as it is badly split and a major contributor to the hump in the deck.*
> *Requires extensive refastening and painting.*
> *Otherwise in fair condition.*

In the following months Bob took off her lines and corrected her stem by making and fitting a new stem fashioned from a local oak tree. In order to jack the deck back into line, he removed the cockpit coaming and the king plank. Once the deck was back where it should be, he installed a new kingplank and reinstalled the original coaming. Next he refastened her planks, then handed me sandpaper, paint, and a brush.

When *Shadow* was back together, painted, and in the water Bob took photographs to show to Fletcher Lewis, a retired Stratford, Con-

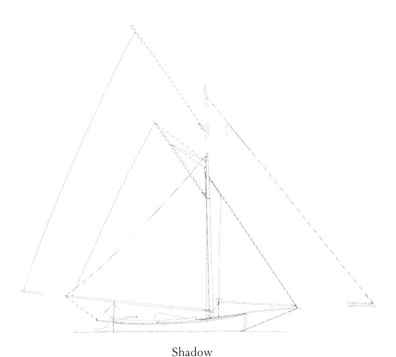

Shadow
LOA: 21' ½"; Beam: 9' 11 ¼"
Measured and drawn by RHB; note racing rig outline behind working rig.

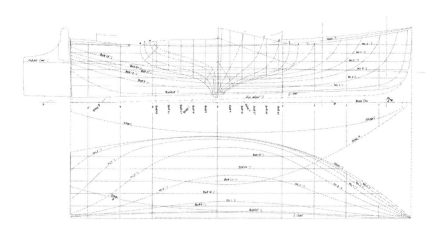

necticut, harbormaster, and a Stratford resident. Lewis, we had learned, knew a great deal about the history of sandbaggers. Bob showed him the photographs of *Shadow* and asked him if he had ever seen this boat.

"Sure," Lewis said. "That's *Shadow* without a stick of ballast in her!"—and he was right.

Although Fletcher was in his nineties, not only did he have an amazing memory but he could recall the comprehensive history of many sandbaggers, including *Shadow*.

We learned that *Shadow* had been built by William Robbins in 1906; Fletcher had photos of her being built in Stratford, her racing history, and even a list of her four previous owners.

Shadow's first owners of record were the Bradley twins, Ernest and Irving, of Westport, Connecticut. In 1914, just before the First World War, *Shadow* was stored under a stack of salt hay to protect her from the sun. The hay, with its heavy salt content, retained moisture and acted as a natural preservative. In 1932, Frederick Ventulette, an oysterman and the last owner before Dr. Teuscher, freed *Shadow* from under the hay and converted her to a "natural-growth' oyster sloop. At that time in Connecticut, the state-owned, natural-growth oyster beds could only be worked by sail-powered dredgers. *Shadow*'s rig was reduced in size to be more manageable, and she was renamed *Bobby*. She worked the natural oyster beds in the Bridge-port/Stratford area and the private oyster grounds off Southport and Norwalk, Connecticut, from 1932 to 1942. In 1942, she was sold to Dr. Teuscher, re-named *Shadow*, and for the next twenty-three years she was part of the Teuscher family.

Shadow's sails and spars no longer existed, but with photographs and records of the spar dimensions of the 21-foot sandbagger *E. Z. Sloat,* the same size as *Shadow*, Bob was able to reconstruct *Shadow*'s working rig and from that, her racing rig.

Bob was delighted with *Shadow* the first time he sailed her. "This enormous thing can actually sail!" he said. We were using her working rig with a slightly larger headsail, but her working rig was big enough! Her desire to "take off" worried us a couple of times, especially when we had the kids aboard. Bob felt she sailed quite well, was responsive, quick, and a good boat.

In 1968 we delivered *Shadow* to Douglas, who would keep her on a mooring in Jamestown, Rhode Island. However, *Shadow* never was sailed and nine years later, Douglas donated *Shadow* to the South Street Seaport in New York City. The museum sent their steel schooner *Pioneer* to pick her up, and she was loaded by crane off the end of a wharf in Jamestown and onto *Pioneer*'s deck.

"If she had to go," Bob said, "I was glad to see her leave on the back of another sailing ship."

Gordon Douglas was an exceptional client. He was not a sailor, and it was obvious he would never sail *Shadow*, but because of his sincere interest in saving an important old boat he had given Bob a rare opportunity to study a sandbagger, research her history, take off her lines, and find out how well she performed under sail.

During our visit with Fletcher Lewis in Stratford, we had discovered another old boat. Pulling her rotting tarp aside, it was clear that at one time she, too, had been a beautiful sandbagger. Named *Tam O'Shanter*, she was built in the late 1800s. We learned she had raced for some years under her big rig, then went working under a reduced rig. Originally the same size as *Shadow*, her stern had been lengthened a foot, an engine had been installed, and a cabin had been built over her deck. Otherwise she appeared to be in sound condition.

After surveying *Tam O'Shanter*, Bob called Gordon Douglas and they drove to Connecticut to take a look. Bob was anxious to get the boat into his own yard, since he felt there was so much more he could learn. He quoted Douglas a price of $3,800 that included her transportation to Warren and restoring her to her original appearance, including her sails, spars, and rigging. Douglas agreed to have her transported to Warren, but didn't feel he could handle owning another boat so he gave her to Bob to do with as he wished.

We didn't have the means to restore her, but that didn't stop Bob from studying her closely. He found out where her centerboard had been, and after poking and prodding, he felt her construction matched most of the sandbaggers that he had looked at. When Bob was satisfied with what he had learned, he contacted Havilah Hawkins, who had a powered oyster dredger in Camden, Maine, whose plan it was to rebuild *Tam O'Shanter* and go racing. Instead,

Tam O'Shanter

Bob heard that Hawkins sold the boat to Paul Bates of Noank, Connecticut, who donated her to a museum in France.
Years later I received this letter from Gordon Douglas:

When I saw Bob's shop, the work he was doing, and the old tools he used, I knew Baker was the right man to restore our boating heritage.
    I have never disagreed with Bob's judgment. By the time he was ready to discuss a project, he was sure of what he would say and would commence to explain everything in great detail. Bob's philosophy of life was that by which he lived and brought to the material things he worked with. He would study a boat for several months before touching it, and only then would begin restoration, guided by what he had learned. He believed in doing only what was absolutely necessary and erring, if anything, to the side of restoring rather than replacing wherever possible. I think that is how he got people going, got them interested, because they could feel his intense thoughts and see a consistent approach.

Traveling the coast back and forth to Stratford also meant exploring numerous boatyards along the way. One day, instead of the usual route we decided to take the ferry to Greenport, New York, at the

Ariel
LOA: 31′0″; Beam: 13′0″

eastern end of Long Island, then head west to City Island, an island known since 1761 as a home to ships. After City Island, we would do a U-turn and head back to Stratford—except we never got any farther than Greenport because Bob discovered yet another sandbagger. This one was different. It was a watch-boat, a type of sandbagger he had heard about but had never seen.

We spent the night!

Early the next morning Bob was back at the docks. He talked to various people until he found a fisherman who knew about her history. *Ariel* was built in 1882 as a watch boat for the oyster industry in Norwalk, Connecticut, specifically to protect the oyster beds from poachers, the fisherman told him, and they went aboard.

"*Ariel*," Bob explained, "looked like a typical sandbagger—slack bilge, plum stem and stern—but her construction was much heavier. It enabled her to stand on her feet without a large crew, while her huge rig gave her the capability of moving fast in light air." When we discovered her, she still had sails but her boom had been shortened, an engine installed, and a cabin built over her deck.

Bob felt that a great many of the boats regarded as genuine sandbaggers were not ones at all, and he wondered how many of them were actually fitted with the extreme rig of the racing sandbagger.

Perhaps," he reiterated, "there is a romantic tendency today to look at a great, wide skimming dish and say, 'Ah, sandbagger!' But is it, in fact, even moderately safe to assume that they are indeed sandbaggers? That isn't to say that some weren't raced as sandbaggers at one time or another, but how do you decide which were and which were not?"

To Bob, the term sandbagger indicated the extreme rig as well as the shifting ballast. "In my younger days" he said, "we occasionally took moveable ballast along to keep some of our improbable boats right side up! So maybe that made them sandbaggers too!"

Bob's knowledge of sandbaggers had spread to Albany, New York. James F. Sefcik, curator of history at New York State Museum in Albany, had written to Maynard Bray at Mystic Seaport, hoping to find somebody who could tell them about a sandbagger named *Sandy* that had been donated to the State History Collection and was in need of restoration.

Bray replied to Sefcik, "Bob Baker is regarded by Mystic Seaport as the foremost authority on sandbaggers. He is the only man known to have actually restored these boats. He is a talented designer and his draftsmanship is superb."

It wasn't long after that that Bob received a letter from Sefcik asking if he could visit Bob's shop and bring pictures of the sandbagger named *Sandy*.

That was in 1971. Sefcik was sure Bob was the right choice but he would need to contact additional marine historians and architects before the state would make a decision as to who would be hired. It would take four years before Bob got the job to execute a lines drawing and sail plan for *Sandy*. He was delighted and anxious to study the boat and act as a consultant for her restoration. Bob felt that *Sandy* was an important, rather pretty boat and one of the oldest racing sandbaggers available for study. She was also unusual enough to raise a number of interesting questions.

"The shape is certainly representative of the type and age," Bob said, and felt her building date was fairly close. The construction—what was left of the original—and her short counter stern, he felt, "was of great interest and most unusual!" But was she a racing sandbagger?

Sandy was built around 1855 in New York City, allegedly by George Darling. She is a gaff-rigged modified racing sloop with a counter stern, a single mast, and a flat keel, one of the last flat-keeled boats of this type, and originally sailed on Lake Cazenovia in upstate New York.

As the story goes, the owners had bad luck sailing the boat and as a result she sat in a boathouse unused for many years. She was then sold to a university football coach, who sold her to a group of Syracuse University football players, who took the boat to Skaneateles, New York. Later, abandoned by the students, *Sandy* was pastured in a bean field to be rescued at auction by the Knauth family of Skaneateles in the early 1950s. They sailed the then ninety-five-year-old boat until the early 1970s when she was donated to the New York State Museum, complete with her original suit of sails. The name "W. Darling, Sailmaker, City Island, N.Y." was marked on the sails. The sailmaker was the brother of her builder.

Sandy had been referred to as a sandbagger, but Bob questioned this. Her design and sailing abilities seemed to him borderline. Correspondence indicated that she had a reputation as a poor sailer. While measuring the boat, Bob discovered three different waterlines: one was scribed, and two were painted. When Bob balanced the rig against the hull, he found that the center of effort of the sails was much too far aft. One of the original owners had apparently tried to fix this by ballasting the stern, but this brought the bow up until she blew around badly.

"No wonder she had a bad reputation!" Bob said, and traced this problem to the scribed waterline found under the paint and located approximately 4 inches above the keel at the stem.

"This painted waterline, was created after the mast broke and the rig was shortened in 1950, and she probably balanced a little better then," he explained, but he felt it probable that *Sandy*'s builder intended her to float deeper—on a waterline about a foot above the keel. Bob felt that, trimmed like this, she could have been made to sail satisfactorily by either moving the rig forward or the centerboard aft, both expensive operations. "Perhaps this is the reason she has

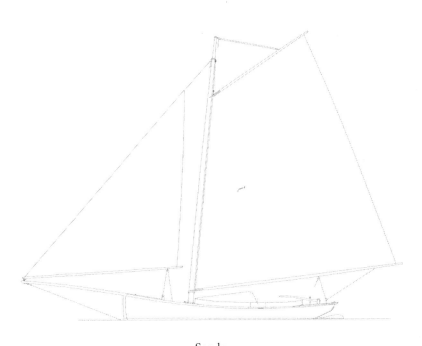

Sandy
LOA: 19'6"; Beam: 7'9¾"
Measured and drawn by RHB

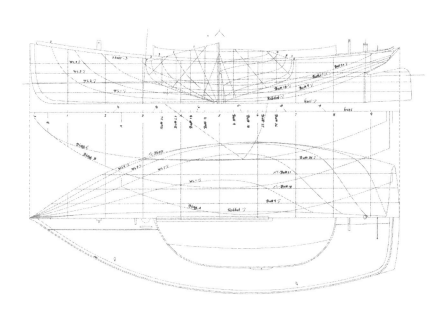

lasted so long," he said. "Being a bad-actor, she was not sailed much, and therefore not strained and driven apart."

Bob wondered if George Darling was a "backyard builder" and had designed the boat after contemporary practice of the times. "But I don't want to be too hard on Darling for confusing the centers of effort and plane. Unless this is your life's work, it's a very difficult thing to estimate from a builder's model without first laying it all out on paper, which most builders didn't do in those days."

Bob felt *Sandy* was a pretty boat, and her drawings could be fixed to correct the balance. "However, before any work is done on her, she should be measured and a complete set of lines and construction details drawn. I'm a great believer in going slow—make sure you're right before starting conservation," he advised.

Sandy was in a good state of repair, except for some drying out as a consequence of the varnish having been stripped off the hull. Raw wood, with or without humidity, wasn't Bob's idea of a good thing and he advised using raw linseed oil and turpentine, half and half. This he said, "would soak into the wood, not change the color any more than varnish and would not prevent the future use of varnish." But, he advised, "in all cases synthetic varnish should be avoided."

Because *Sandy* hadn't been properly cradled, Bob was concerned when he noticed places on her hull where the stern had been allowed to drop due to the hull being incorrectly supported. Bob was anxious to see that problem corrected before the boat lost her original shape. His advice was taken, a new cradle was designed, constructed, and in place in no time.

Bob took *Sandy*'s lines. She was then repaired following Bob's instructions and is now on permanent display in the Urban Recreation section of the New York Metropolis Exhibit in Albany, New York.

Bob never did decide if she was or wasn't a racing sandbagger.

Contributions: Benjamin A. G. Fuller; Gordon Douglas; James F. Sefcik; Maynard Bray.

A Launch

Bluebird was her name. She had a graceful sensuous shape and was a delight to look at from the moment she was trailed into our yard by a client who was anxious to get her repaired and in the water. She even looked a bit hoity-toity, as if she didn't realize she looked so disheveled and un-groomed. As if a blight had struck, her topsides were thick with mold, and both garboard planks had fallen off. Fortunately for Bob, bringing her back to life would mean a badly needed temporary reprieve from sandbagger research. *Bluebird*, complete with her original Palmer single-cylinder engine, was built by the Palmer Brothers of Connecticut in the early 1900s.

The Palmer Brothers mainly built engines but they also built launches to use as stock boats and as vehicles for their engines. Because the Palmer Brothers churned out so many of these launches, it meant that the boats had to be quickly and cheaply built with minimum finish.

BLUEBIRD
LOA: 17'0"; Beam: 4'8 ½"
Measured and drawn by RHB

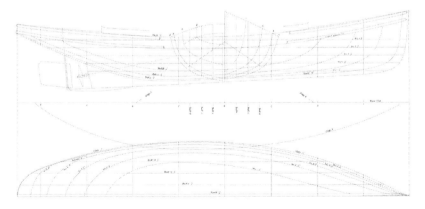

Bob moved *Bluebird* into the shop, and after supporting all her important points, he began to poke and prod as usual. Except for her missing garboard planks, she was in good condition structurally. "Just shows you can't compare the virgin wood we had back in 1900s to today's fast-grown trees." The *Bluebird* is privately owned.

Photographs: Personal collection.

Woods Hole Spritsail Boats

The door to a Cape Cod boat shop located in Woods Hole, Massachusetts, hadn't been opened since 1913. Inside were two rare craft known as Woods Hole spritsail boats, their condition as good as the day the shop door was closed. The boats had been built by a lifetime resident of the village named Edward E. Swift (1862–1964), a carpenter and cabinetmaker who built houses, barns, and even fine furniture, but who never before had built a boat. His purpose in building the boats was simply to see if he could build a better one. And he did.

Swift built his first boat in the 1890s and named her *Spy*. It's thought that Swift gave her away or sold her. In 1896 Swift built a second boat, and named her *Susie* after his wife. *Susie* must have been a better design than *Spy,* since she was a consistent winner in local races. This second attempt bears testimony to Eddie's ability as a boatbuilder.

It was clear that Eddie Swift never duplicated an existing design in building these boats. He started from scratch, using a time-honored method. He made a model, took the lines off the model, and followed with full-size molds and patterns around which he created his craft. The result was a boat quite similar in general characteristics to the spritsail boats already well known in Woods Hole, but through his craftsmanship and his meticulous attention to detail, Eddie Swift built a better boat.

By 1914 Swift built a third boat for his brother, Helon. Only the finishing touches remained to be completed when Helon died. Eddie, stricken with grief, lost interest in the boat, and closed and locked the door of his shop.

For many years Bob had been interested in the Woods Hole spritsail boats—a workingman's craft used for fishing and lobstering, and later, racing. His research had suggested that the Newport fish and lobster boats, such as *Button Swan*, had a connection, perhaps as cousins—both types built in the 12- to 13-foot range, and essentially undecked.

To reach the fishing grounds, a boat like *Button Swan* had the advantage of open water, while a Woods Hole boat had to contend with considerable current, stone bridges too low to sail under, and to be able to row when the wind died out. To compensate for these conditions, Woods Hole boats were built heavier, with higher topsides, a narrower beam for easier rowing, and instead of a gaff rig like *Button Swan*'s, the Woods Hole boats used a boomless spritsail This rig enabled the fisherman to quickly lower the sail to pass under a bridge, and on reaching the other side, put the oars away and easily raise the rig again.

When Swift died at the age of 101, his possessions were inherited by his grandniece, Mrs. John E. White. This included *Susie*. Mrs. White gave the unnamed boat to Mystic Seaport. By 1969 the Whites were planning to move, which meant they would have to part with *Susie*. While wondering how to find her the right home, the Whites saw an article about us and our boats. Soon after reading the article, Mr. White wrote Bob a letter explaining his need to find a home for an ancient Woods Hole boat named *Susie* that had been designed and built by his great-uncle Edward E. Swift. Bob knew about the Woods Hole spritsail boats. He had studied the nameless one at Mystic, but he had never seen *Susie*, only heard about her. He immediately wrote back, suggesting a date that we could take a look.

Two weeks later we arrived at the Whites' house. *Susie*, her cockpit covered with a tarp, was comfortably perched on the lawn. Bob was so excited when he saw her name, I thought he'd chew his pipe stem in half.

The Whites greeted us warmly, and while Mrs. White was telling stories about sailing the boat, Mr. White untied and removed the tarp. Bob stuck his head into the boat, nodding with pleasure as he studied her from forward to aft, then straightened up, and smiled at me.

Mr. White, pointing to his lawn chairs, gestured to us to come and sit down. We enjoyed coffee and donuts while Mrs. White told us about the spritsail boats. She explained that in the beginning,

around the 1870s, the spritsail boats were used only for fishing and lobstering until the wealthy summer residents took note of them and in no time decided it would be fun to arrange a race among the fishermen that included cash prizes for the winners.

"The races were great fun," she said, "and before long, the summer residents wanted boats of their own to race, and by 1897, the Woods Hole Yacht Club had been established."

At this point Bob was looking a bit apprehensive. Plans for *Susie*'s future had not been resolved. Five more minutes passed. Mr. White, took a sip of his coffee, looked at Bob and announced, "Come take the boat at your earliest opportunity. It would mean a great deal to us to know that *Susie* would be in good hands. And as for the $200 you offered," White said, "let that come as it will."

A week later, *Susie*, built in 1896, was happily cradled in front of our boatshop.

After Bob cleaned off the dust and dirt and aired out her sails, he launched *Susie* and took her for a sail and came to quickly understand why she was a champion.

She held her course and moved like a dream, doing exactly what he asked of her. And when he was done with his own trials and had taken her measurements, she received new paint, her interior and decks were oiled, and Bob enjoyed sailing her for a number of years.

After studying the two Swift boats—*Susie* and the nameless one at Mystic—there was no doubt in Bob's mind that each had been an improvement over the previous one, and that's what Bob wanted to study—he wanted to get inside Ed Swift's head. If Bob could find *Spy*, the first boat Ed Swift built, he would have all three boats to study and perhaps be able to unlock Swift's mind, revealing his ideas and secrets.

A few years later, when sniffing around Tripp's Boatyard in Westport, Bob spotted a derelict fiberglass hull lying on the beach. "That's *Spy*," he said, " I know it."

"Okay," I said. I wasn't about to argue. Obviously Bob was hallucinating. The boat looked as sick as a beached whale. Not to Bob. He had to have it, but the owner, a fisherman, wasn't interested in selling. A year went by, and the owner still wouldn't cooperate, so I said, let me try. Using my feminine charms, in no time I got him to agree to sell it to me for twenty-five bucks—AND without any conditions.

Fearing he'd change his mind, I raced home, told Bob, and we hitched up our trailer, and in no time we had the derelict offloaded and into the shop. Bob freed her of her fiberglass coffin, then shined a flashlight across her transom, hoping to find her name. Bob knew that Swift used brass letters attached with screws to the transom. And yes, Bob was right. He had found *Spy*. Along with the screw holes that had secured the brass letters was a perfect impression of the name *Spy*. Bob finally had access to all three of Swift's Woods Hole spritsail boats to study.

When Bob asked me to strip out *Spy*'s twentieth-century alter-ations, I was delighted. Having recorded the lives of many old houses and their changes, I was deeply involved in archaeology so this wasn't a new adventure, except instead of being a house, it was a boat—above-ground archaeology, I called it

As I carefully stripped out the twentieth-century junk, I began to find many of her original details—knees, centerboard, thwart loca-tions, paint and varnish, and even her bronze mast gate—years of her history.

Seaworthy conservation was out of the question. Due to rot, 90 percent of her original pieces would have to be replaced. Bob con-tacted the curator of the Woods Hole Historical Museum, told him that *Spy* had been found, explained her condition, and said that he would like to donate the boat to the museum. The curator said, "Yes, this is where *Spy* belongs."

Out of her fiberglass coffin, *Spy* was now so weak that she could easily fall apart while making the trip by land from Westport to the

Woods Hole Museum. For that reason and for display, Bob made an outside mold, set her inside, and put me to work installing some sister frames. When finished, her topsides sparkling with a fresh coat of paint, she now held her own and was delivered safely to the Woods Hole Museum—Eddie Swift's first Woods Hole spritsail boat was back home.

My heart quivers with awe when I realize how many boats Bob has rescued, looked at, listened to, and figured out who and why they were. As he always said, "It would be a wobbly future for maritime history without finding the souls of workingmen's boats."

Contributions: *Skipper Magazine* 1968. H. V. R. Palmer.
Photographs: Personal collection.

Moving

After two years of living on the second floor of our oyster building, we were yearning for open space. We began to look at ads for a farmhouse in Westport, Massachusetts, and soon discovered a two-story house built circa 1700. It seemed perfect, except for the farmer who had previously made an offer for the sixty-acre property. It turned out that he wanted the land but not the house. "Fine," Bob said. "We'll take the house and move it to an area not useful for farming." The farmer agreed.

The house needed a major overhaul inside and out. We had a foundation to finish, structural repairs to make, window sashes to replace, a chimney top to rebuild, asbestos siding to remove, roof and walls to shingle, and trim to paint. Five fireplaces needed re-pointing. Sheets of plywood covering the original floorboards had to be pulled up. There was wallpaper and peeling paint to strip off, woodwork to patch, plumbing, heating, and electricity to install.

And then we began to collect more buildings. We had barely begun work on the house when Bob was told about a shed in Marsh-

Another building arrives to become the ell of the main house

field, Massachusetts, slated for demolition. A shed is a shed but not this one. It had belonged to a shipbuilder and was the only remaining building on the site of a pre-Revolutionary shipyard. Naturally Bob had to have it. It took three days to dismantle and move to Westport and another week to reassemble.

Next to come was a Cape Cod house that Bob would use for his shop; next, an eighteenth-century slaughterhouse for use for storage; another shed that Bob had to have; moving and attaching an ell; and naturally a barn; followed by a seventeenth-century Rhode Island one-room stone-ender. All of the above were dismantled, moved, and re-erected. We created Bakerville—a place where the past had become part of the present

Somehow, despite adopting buildings, we had managed to keep working on the house. By the end of October we had rebuilt the chimney top, shingled the roof and walls, and even painted the trim. The house looked radiant.

Bakerville 1975

I had never thought about what makes an old house glow until Bob said, "Like boats, it was designed and built by instinct, not by architects. The shape, the size, the individual details have been created by gut feeling and need. The windows, trim, doors, and chimney top, and even each pane of glass are in perfect proportion with the overall proportions of the house. Something the old-time builders knew how to do and today is forgotten."

Bob didn't care whether it was a boat, a house, a car, or a tool that needed repair as long as it was worthy of respect. For Bob conservation meant preserving the past.

"Keep it simple," he'd say.

And he definitely taught me the value of handsaws, miter boxes, hand planes, hand drills, chisels, etc. No machinery meant delightful quietness while working together.

The 1975 New England bi-centennial had brought new hope for ancient buildings and my old house contracting business became very busy, With the children in school, I was gone throughout the day. I don't know if Bob felt lonely—who knows—but he began to have girlfriends. First one, then another, then a serious one, and we lived separate lives for a number of years. I thought that if we could restore boats, houses, and just about everything else, we could definitely restore our marriage. It wasn't easy, as neither of us had the tools. It took time, but we found them.

Photographs: Personal collection.

Ancient Boats

Bob had had an opportunity in 1974, back in his Warren shop, to research *Button Swan*, built circa 1870, and *Peggotty* built circa 1850. Classified as primitive, Newport fish and lobster boats were in existence before 1840, but little had been recorded concerning their heritage.

When Bob was fourteen, he read a newspaper article about the *Button Swan*'s discovery and learned that after years of fishing, *Button* had been put to rest in a barn in Saunderstown, Rhode Island, where she was found by Alfred S. Brownell, a noted authority on sailing vessels. Brownell, realizing her importance, convinced the owner to donate the boat to Mystic Seaport.

Maynard Bray, in his book, *Mystic Seaport Museum Watercraft*, wrote about *Button Swan*:

> *Historically the* Button Swan *is unique. She is a well-preserved, well-documented example of a small working catboat with roots reaching back 125 years or more. She was made by a man who is known to have built boats of this very type at Newport over 100 years ago. This man was William Henry Munroe, better known as Button Swan. Button was born in 1833 and died in 1905, a respected boat builder and fisherman. Button was so named because he was short of stature and the Swan was added because his uncle John Swan was a close friend since youth. The boat* Button Swan, *named after him, was built by Button for his good friend Captain Fernando Fowler of Wickford, Rhode island, who named it* Button Swan.... *Certainly no existing catboat in the Mystic Seaport collection or elsewhere can equal her importance.*

Due to the boat's importance, Mystic Seaport planned to restore

her and in 1974, the Catboat Association agreed to help finance the project. Bob was chosen to do the work. His restoration skills would include those of a detective, archaeologist, physicist, woodworker, and marine architect—plus lots of patience—all which, fortunately, he possessed. Working with Bob on this project was an apprentice named Kevin Dwyer, who after working with Bob for a number of years, would go on to work at Mystic Seaport as a shipwright.

With the boat in Bob's shop, the customary first step for Bob was to do nothing or so it seemed to anybody who observed him walking around the boat as if he was sanding the floor, his arms crossed, and sucking on his pipe. For Bob this was a critical time. Walking around the boat meant getting acquainted with every part of her. It took a couple of weeks, Bob recalled. "Where she was out of shape, I would take a half-turn on a clamp to close up a station or let a screw in to ease her."

He also relied on historical records, photos, two models, and two measured drawings of the boat, along with the original newspaper story about her discovery.

Button Swan was a typical Newport fish and lobster boat, he reported. They were open with narrow washboards and curbing, and instead of a centerboard they had a wide deep keel. Beamy, with lots of deadrise and low freeboard, they were capable of carrying large catches of fish in the fish well located between the two middle thwarts. A third thwart was located in the bow. Forward of this was the single mast, which was held in place by a hinged iron clamp allowing easy removal of the mast for rowing and sculling. A gaff-headed cat rig was used with a single halyard and mainsheet. A jib

Newport fish and lobster boat

could be added in light weather with the addition of a bowsprit. A distinctive and decorative touch was the wide wale strake with its double guards painted in contrasting colors. But in order to restore *Button Swan*, Bob would need to scrape back layer after layer of paint to determine just where or what her original components had been: fish well, thwarts, rig, type of fastenings, and paint colors.

After Bob had completed his survey and taken measurements and drawn her lines, he was ready to lay out the fish well, the original having been replaced by a gasoline engine. With the floors removed from the well area and the thwarts cleaned off, Bob was able to deter-

Button Swan, *circa 1870*
LOA: 12' 4"; Beam 5' 2¾"
Measured and drawn by RHB

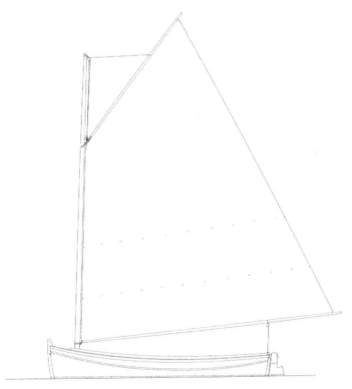

Rig reconstructed from photographs. Some boats of this type carried a small jib set flying from a removable bowsprit. There is no evidence that this boat was fitted with a jib.

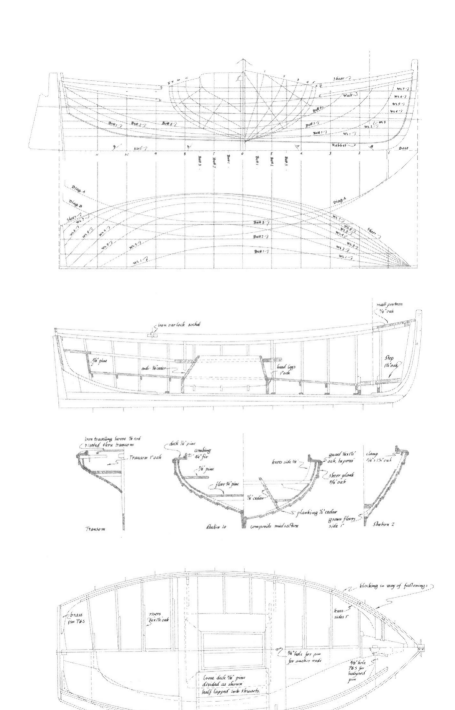

mine the exact location and the size of the well. The new well would be built as a unit outside the boat, but installing it meant removing both thwarts. The end of one knee on the after thwart fell off when he moved the thwart.

"The knee had been broken for a long time," he told me, "and was full of dirt and lots of paint. While trying to salvage it with lots of epoxy I got the distinct impression that Button was sitting back on his heels laughing at the idea of modern fixer-uppers."

Bob also discovered that the two 'midship side benches were originally part of the deck that butted against the fish well. Under the main thwart, on the ceiling, Bob found marks of a small cleat each side. "I feel that they were used to hold a parting board against the thwart knee."

He noted that there was a hole in the forward thwart for a pin and felt this was used to make up the anchor rode. There was some wear on the forward edge of the thwart as from rope, and no evidence of cleats anywhere else for securing the anchor rode.

When *Button Swan* was acquired by Mystic Seaport, her rig had long since disappeared. Determined to reconstruct the original on paper, Bob relied on old photographs and evidence he found in the boat. "Forward of the third thwart was the single mainmast, which was held in place by a hinged iron clamp, confirming that a gaff-headed cat-rig was used with a single halyard and mainsheet."

Bob discovered that the fastenings were a combination of iron and yellow metal. "The two didn't react on one another particularly and the iron hardly rusted, as it was Swedish iron—good, old-fashioned wrought iron." As far has Bob knew, the yellow metal had not been analyzed. "It is not brass. There is no sign of crystallization or deterioration. Although it is too hard for riveting it can be clenched." Yellow metal nails were used for fastening the laps in the planks also, and again, they were imperfectly clinched.

After Bob had removed enough of the boat's interior, he was able to obtain reliable paint samples from areas where the paint had never been removed. Analyzing the paint was a slow and painstaking job. "It's a miserable undertaking," Bob recalled, "but rewarding." He found that the dominant color was salmon, a color he referred to as "Band-Aid pink." This was the original color that Button used, Bob

felt, explaining, "Later it was followed by Tuscan red, yellow ochre, and gray. The wide wale with its double guards painted in contrasting colors was a distinctive and decorative touch."

Methodically, by scraping away the layers, Bob had found *Button Swan*'s past: how she was built, how she was used, and the colors she had been painted—or, you might say, the clothes she wore.

"I had a ball with that boat." Bob said. "I knew who built her and when she was built and there are so few boats that you really know about. So when I was working in his boat and I'd come to something, I'd say, 'Button what in heaven's name did you do that for,' and the deeper I looked, damn if he didn't tell me."

I can imagine Button Swan looking at Bob's calloused and bruised hands, shaking his head while wondering why anybody would think his boat so special.

Photograph: Mystic Seaport Museum.

Shortly after completing the conservation of *Button Swan*, Bob was again hired by Mystic Seaport to document and take a set of lines off another Newport fish and lobster boat named *Peggotty*. She was the only other surviving fish and lobster boat and an important follow-up to *Button Swan*. Again the Catboat Association agreed to help finance the project.

I remember it was a cold, cheerless day, the day I went to Little Compton to bring Bob hot coffee and a sandwich and to see how he was doing measuring *Peggotty*. He instantly wrapped his fingers around the hot mug; then after swallowing a bite of the peanut butter

1920s postcard of Peggotty

and jelly sandwich (his standby), he showed me what he was finding. "Frustrating though," he said. "trying to take the lines off a boat with a house on top."

"But better than diving 150 feet to take the lines off a sunken ship." I said, and received a twisted smile in reply.

Peggotty has a strange and interesting history. She was of the same type as *Button Swan* but was now a permanent exhibit at the Wilbor House—the Little Compton Historical Society's headquarters—last used, not as a boat, but as a studio for artist Sidney Burleigh.

Bob, as usual, was intrigued by her construction, which was heavier but also identical to *Button Swan*'s. Her history was even more amazing. After twenty-five years of fishing, *Peggotty* went into service as a ferry, carrying produce and passengers between Providence, Little Compton, and Middletown. A frequent passenger was a local artist named Sidney Burleigh, who for years had taken this ferry from Providence to his summerhouse in Little Compton. Many years later, *Peggoty* was left abandoned on a Little Compton beach, and it wasn't until 1906 that Burleigh discovered her bones, and in a flush of passion and inspiration, carted her remains to his summer home in Little Compton and planted her in his back garden. Burleigh proceeded to turn *Peggotty* into his tearoom and studio. He attached a wall of planks to the gunwales, cut a door through, installed enough

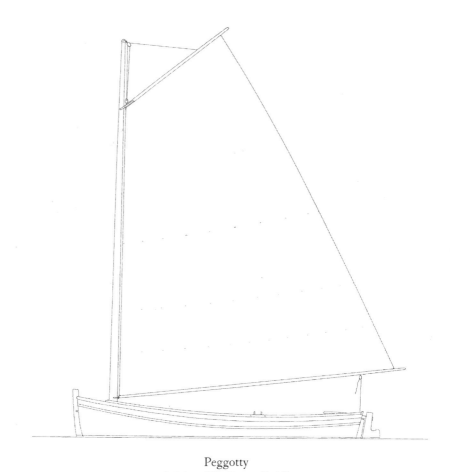

Peggotty
LOA: 17′6″; Beam: 8′9¾″
Measured and drawn by RHB
Probable rig. Reconstructed from contemporary engravings and related material.

windows to give him light, and topped it all with a thatched roof. Finished, he named his studio *Peggotty*—a studio often referred to as a nautical haystack.

When Burleigh died in 1931, his boat/studio was again left untended until 1964, when Burleigh's wife donated *Peggotty* to the Little Compton Historical Society. When the boat/studio was moved, her keel was left behind, and without it her only support became timbers placed under the planking. Eventually the planks pushed up, changing the shape of the bottom. Bob explained that despite this problem

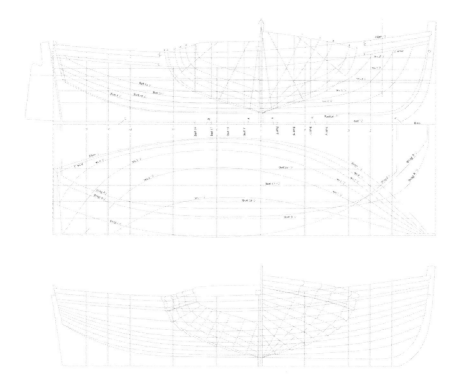

he was able to get a good set of measurements from the topsides down to the waterline, and for the depth of the hull he measured to the bottom of the original fish well.

The thwarts were missing, but most of her original structure, the frames, floor timbers, and knees remained although some were out of position or broken. The hole for the mast was still there, but again, Bob would have to depict the rig based on period engravings of Newport Harbor. The paint colors were inconclusive, the only traces of pre-Burleigh paint being bits of green copper in the planking laps. The oldest paint in her interior was yellow ochre with some traces of salmon on the remaining thwart knees.

Sadly, the Little Compton Historical Society still doesn't recognize the importance of what they have. There is no doubt it's a whimsical structure, but their exhibit label barely mentions her true heritage as a Newport lobster and fish boat long before she became an artist's studio. "Folly has transpired over reason," Bob commented. Bob was interested in any old working boat. Not for comparison with a modern boat, but for what it was—what the early men thought about and anticipated when designing and building a boat.

Taking off *Peggotty*'s lines had involved lots of investigation and speculation. "Much of the work was like a puzzle and just as exciting when the pieces worked," Bob wrote. But there were some teasers that only could be answered by building another *Peggotty*. "This," Bob said, "would be a learning experience, to say the least. "

When a customer came by wanting a character boat built, Bob suggested *Peggotty*. He was hired, and after Bob and his apprentice Kevin Dwyer finished building the new *Peggotty* in 1977, a detailed article about the project was published in *WoodenBoat* No. 23.

Bob was anxious to see how *Peggotty* would sail. "To tell the truth, I didn't know what to expect of the old girl. With her long keel and broad beam, I knew she wasn't about to sail herself, and yes, I discovered she had to be sailed. The old Newport fishermen were known as expert sailors, and it was this skill that made them successful fishermen, judging the tides and getting their boats in and out of the rocky ledges as the boat and the man worked together."

Peggotty's owner was posted overseas, so the boat spent several years at Mystic Seaport and for several years became part of the WoodenBoat School fleet. She's once again at Mystic.

Today's young students learning how to sail are taught the words; port, starboard, bow, stern, rudder, tiller, jib and sheet and how they are used, but little about the need for the boat and skipper to work together. I was thinking of this on a very stormy day, a day I was walking on the beach and noticed a small gaff-rigged boat trying to get through the gut that led into the harbor. The waves were tremendous. As I watched in fear, I began to see that the boat and the skip-

per were working together. The skipper knew what to ask of the boat, the boat knew how to respond, and working together they arrived safely in the harbor.

Photographs: Bob Foley, Shirley Utterback, *Providence Journal*, and personal collection.

In 1978 Bob discovered *Rescue*, a rowing boat built in 1869 that had recently been donated to the Newport Historical Society, where she was on display. She was not a true Newport fish and lobster boat, but had some of the same features—a clinker-built hull, but heavily quartered like a typical Newport fish and lobster boat. When Bob first saw her, he was delighted, since she certainly was a part of the evolution of the Newport boats.

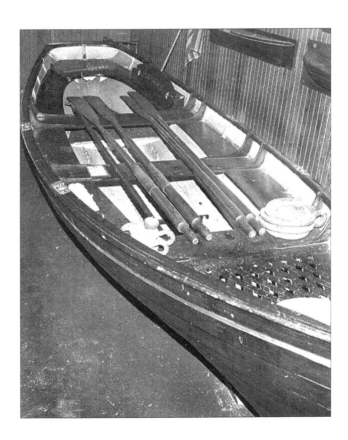

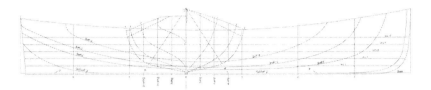

Rescue
LOA: 13′11″; Beam: 4′3″
Measured and drawn by RHB

"Because she was an interesting and pretty boat, I took off her lines." In no time he was given the opportunity to research her history. "A hell of a lot happened in Newport," Bob said. "I think you can probably make a whole in-depth study of the influences. *Rescue* is well documented and although she is in poor condition she is available for study. In this case we know who built her and why."

Rescue had belonged to Ida Lewis and was reportedly built by Thomas Stoddard at Long Wharf in Newport. Ida's father was keeper of Lime Rock Light in the Newport Harbor, the present location of the Ida Lewis Yacht Club. When Ida was fifteen, her father suffered a stroke and it fell on her to continue the task of keeping the lighthouse, which often meant rescues at sea from her small rowing boat.

Her most noted rescue was in 1869 when she set out, unaided, in a bitter storm to help two men whose boat had upset in a sudden squall. This daring and successful rescue was heralded around the world and Ida became famous overnight. As a tribute for this heroic deed, the pulling boat *Rescue* was presented to Ida Lewis by the citizens of Rhode Island.

Speculating about the two wooden air tanks, still placed against the ceiling between the thwarts, Bob felt they didn't appear to be of the same workmanship as the boat. "It is doubtful that the builder intended the tanks to be put in and they were perhaps added by Ida to aid in her rescues. Legend has it that Ida Lewis made her daring rescues unaided. However, it is interesting to note that the forward oarlocks show the most wear, indicating one to row and one to steer," and he blatantly added, "So it might be interesting to know who rowed Miss Lewis around—or who did she row around!"

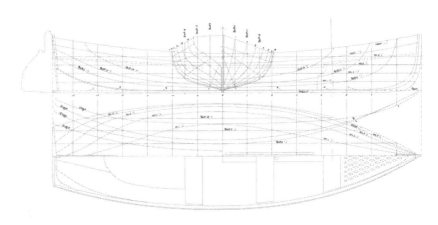

15′ Sailing Whitehall
LOA: 14′10″; Beam: 4′2″
Designed by RHB

The lines of *Rescue* appealed to a friend who was thinking of having a small pulling boat designed and built by Bob. The heavy quarters suited his purpose, but Bob had reservations about the stern. He didn't like the way the lines finished off at the transom. He pointed to the plans to show the hollow at the garboard. "The plank cannot be bent into this without being straight for the width of the plank." So Bob redesigned the boat, making a change in her body plan, and the design became 15-foot Sailing Whitehall.

"I took a little bit of squat out of the quarters, and the 'midship sections are a whisker flatter than the original. I also added a foot to her length," he said. The result was more refined than the original but still had *Rescue*'s stability. In order for the new boat to sail, Bob designed a small spritsail rig and added an off-center centerboard, a concept that had intrigued him ever since he built the off-center centerboard in the *Dragonfly* many years earlier. "Off-center creates more room," he told me.

Photographs: Personal collection.

Teaching

The first issue of *WoodenBoat* magazine was published in 1974. Jon Wilson, the editor, was aware that our historical maritime past was getting lost, and he planned to dedicate the magazine to wooden boats with articles written by builders, designers, restorers and sailors. Bob was delighted. "At last people are thinking about the need that I've been aware of all my life."

Wilson dedicated the magazine to the future of young people, embarking on a career that would not bring them riches, but satisfaction. The timing was perfect. The hippie era had left many young men and women reaching for self-discovery while creating something useful.

Now, many years and many issues later, *WoodenBoat* magazine is still firmly tied to the importance of wooden boats, teaching its readers how to design a boat, restore a boat, build a wooden boat, learn about the different types of wood used, the use and care of tools, and how to appreciate aesthetics—while always helping its readers under-

stand what a beautiful wooden boat is all about.

By 1981, *WoodenBoat* had started a school. Its purpose was to share the skills required to build, own, and use a wooden boat. Bob and his draftsman friend, Dave Dillion, were hired to be the teachers in a class named "Understanding the Lines and Shapes of Boats." Their course included an introduction to taking lines, drafting, lofting, and half-hull modeling.

At the same time, Bob had been working with the students at Lance Lee's Apprenticeshop, originally situated at the Bath Maritime Museum in Bath, Maine, and later moved to Rockland, Maine.

Lance Lee's philosophy was to use old boats that were found or donated to the museum as a reference library to learn how they had stood the test of time, what their wear marks revealed about their use, and to help students become equipped with practical experience while learning all possible about the original builder. "Restoration for the students is a vital term," Lee commented. "It's a practice involving reverence for and study of the past as well as perpetuation of skills and knowledge for the future."

Using a "library" boat as a reference, Bob would guide the students on how to document what they had seen and how to measure a boat and draw its lines.

One day while looking through Lee's collection of small boats, Bob was intrigued by a little clinker-built peapod that Lee had acquired.

Bob described her as a "perfectly beautiful tiny pod." and named her Kids' Pod. Eventually her name was changed to "Small Clinker-Built Peapod." Lance had found her hanging as a restaurant sign on Cape Cod.

Bob felt that she was built around 1885. "She is well thought out and very carefully fitted and nicely detailed. My guess she was built by a good boatwright fairly far to the east. Because of her maple frames, she could have been built in Nova Scotia," Bob explained, "and she may have been a boat built for children."

I asked Bob to explain to me how he determined the age of a boat.

His answer: "Get a bottle of rum and sit down with friends and discuss the whole thing."

That didn't tell me much so I asked if he would compare the type of construction with other boats.

His answer: " Possibly."

That didn't tell me much either. So I asked him if he would compare details that are used to determine the age of a house—such as joinery, nails. saw marks, framing details, etc.

Answer: "Sometimes."

"Would it be the shape, then?"

Kid's Pod
LOA: 12′ 10″; Beam: 3′ 9 ¼″
(Plans available from Maine Maritime Museum as Clinker-Built Peapod)

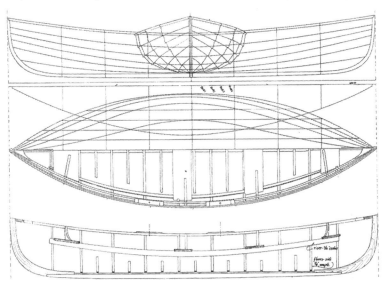

Answer: "Not always."

I kept asking until I understood why he couldn't give me informative answers.

"It's a feeling you get," he said.

I understood. His intuitive perceptions prompted by instinct were impossible to put into words.

There were two other boats in Lee's collection that caught Bob's eyes. One was named *Mollie*; the other was named *Heroma,* built on the same molds as *Mollie* but twenty years later. *Mollie*, a tiny Maine-built Whitehall, was "perfect in all her details and pretty as a picture," according to Bob, and was fitted for sailing. She had no centerboard but did have a rudder.

Mollie was out of shape, and Bob convinced Lee to loan him the boat for a couple of weeks. When *Mollie* arrived at Bob's shop, he did his usual thing of walking around her for a week. Once she was propped back in shape. Bob took her lines off and made notes about her construction, original paint colors, and scantlings.

Bob felt that *Heroma* had been built by the same person on the same molds. "She wasn't as fine as *Mollie*; pretty but not as pretty." The Rockland Apprenticeshop measured her, and Bob drew her lines.

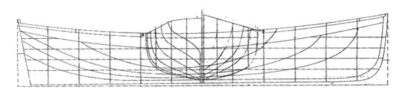

Mollie
LOA: 12'0"; Beam: 3'8"
(Plans available from Maine Maritime Museum as "Whitehall Heroma")

Bob was concerned that there were no historical notes about either of these boats. He felt that these square-sterned Maine boats, as he called them, may be a whole new discovery. Eventually Bob discovered similar types in Bath and Searsport, Maine. But, how, where, and why these square-sterned Maine boats were developed still remains a mystery.

And so is the name "square-sterned boat," because her transom looks like a wine glass. A "square-sterned boat" is simply a Down East Maine term for "transom-sterned."

Photographs: Personal collection.

A Whaleboat

In 1901, the steam whaler *Balaena* was wrecked in a gale near St. Lawrence Island in the Bering Straits. Its whaleboats were rescued and used by Eskimos for twenty-nine years. In 1976, the boats were discovered by the curator of the New Bedford Whaling Museum. Of the thirty whaleboats found at St. Lawrence Island, he chose the two that, due to the cold arctic air, were still in fair condition. When they finally arrived in New Bedford, both boats— referred to as No. 1 and No. 2.—were displayed until No. 1 was moved to Bob's shop for conservation and No. 2 was put into storage.

After ninety years outside, the one in Bob's shop still had the original wear marks, rough hull fairing, and unparalleled framing. Judging from her design and material—cedar, oak, and pine— Bob felt that the boat was originally built around 1890 in Westport or Dartmouth, Massachusetts. Like most nineteenth-century whaleboats, this one had been constructed quickly from pre-cut planks and framing and was only expected to last through a four-year voyage.

Bob's survey showed she had been hit on the port side near the stern, the stem was driven over, her planks were badly splintered and cracked, her cheeks broken, her sheer plank fractured, plus the bow and the stern were hogged, which meant blocking her up on the cribbing, then jacking her a tiny bit each day for several weeks. When she had reached her original shape, the hull planks were refastened.

Bob also felt that she had been damaged in transit, as her trip from the Bering Sea had been difficult. First, she had been placed on a barge; next, she barely survived a small fire. Then she was loaded into a boxcar for the cross-country trip, lost for a couple of weeks in a rail change, and finally arrived at the Whaling Museum in the winter of 1977.

With the help of three apprentices, it took three months of coax-

Whaleboat No. 1, before and after

ing her back into shape, scraping, patching, and painting, in order to restore the boat to what it was originally.

As of this writing, Whaleboat No. 1 is now on exhibit at the New Bedford Whaling Museum.

Contributions: G. S. Sleeman (*Soundings Magazine* 1977).
Photographs: Personal collection.

Skiffs and Sharpies

Even after Bobby became Bob, his interest in skiffs and sharpies never ceased. In 1977 I wasn't surprised to see a rotted and bottomless sharpie, named *Sandpiper*, sitting on sawhorses in his shop. The only thing holding it together was a couple of boards nailed across her middle. *Donoghue* had been in bad shape, but this project was over the top. It didn't matter to Bob, as the boat would give him a chance to measure a fifty-six-year-old sharpie and then repair her.

Sandpiper, *before and after*

Sandpiper, built in 1922, had been sailed for years by Bob's close friend Alden Ring. After years of use, Ring sold the sharpie to a family who used her until her bottom fell off. Even then, her adventures were not over as the family assigned her to shore duty as a sandbox for their children. Later, the father pitched out the sand and brought *Sandpiper* to Bob, confident that Bob could give the boat a new bottom and a new lease on life. Bob was delighted. Ever since childhood he had been researching the skiffs and sharpies once so common to Westport waters and was amazed at how many of these boats kept showing up like long-lost relatives, each one increasing his knowledge about when, how, and who had built the Westport skiffs and sharpies.

The flat-bottomed skiffs and sharpies were very common in and around the Westport River from the late nineteenth century to the present. As Bob said, "They were simply boats, not speed machines,

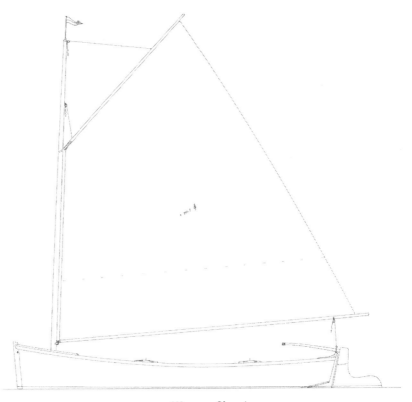

Westport Sharpie
LOA: 14' ¾"; Beam: 4' 11"
Measured and drawn by RHB

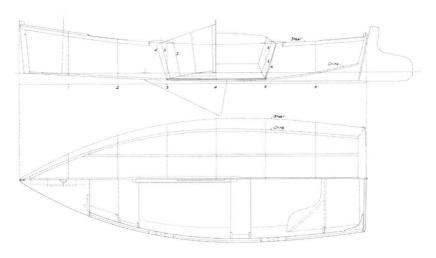

Briggs Shop 1900

stone dragger boats, or racing craft with Whitehall features. They were a poor man's boat: a way to get out on the water for leisure, exercise, fishing, and even romancing."

A Westport Sharpie is built like a Westport Skiff but equipped with a centerboard, sails, and rudder.

Among the most prolific builders of skiffs and sharpies were Fred Tripp and the Briggs family, Christopher (Kit) Briggs and his sons Andrew, Will, and Bert. Bert Briggs (1870-1942) was considered to be the best boatbuilder in Westport. Everything had to be right. If he split a board it had to be replaced by another.

Fred Tripp learned his trade from Bert Briggs, making it difficult to tell their boats apart. However with Bob's careful research on individual boats, he had discovered some distinguishing characteristics. Tripp's boats had hanging knees, a flat top on the stem head and a decorative scroll on the seat riser. Briggs's boats had thwart knees instead of hanging knees and used a two-piece stem that was finished at the top in a pyramid shape.

Westport's skiffs and sharpies are marvelously simple and can be built with basic tools. Skiff and sharpie builders worked from paper patterns of the sides, never from lines and offsets. You begin with the boards that make up the sides, laying them out on the floor, studying their shape, working around the knots, until you end up with the outlines of the sides marked on the boards. As originally built, these boats were simplicity personified. In the early days, the planks used for the topsides were a single piece of pine or cedar. But as time passed and wide pieces became unavailable, the sides were built from two pieces of pine—sometimes overlapped and sometimes butted using the spline-and-glue method. The builders knew instinctively how to shape and set up the stem. The side planks were nailed to the stem, a 'midships mold put in, and the ends of the side planks cranked together at the transom either by muscle or a Spanish windlass, then fastened. The bottom was a series of cross-planked cedar boards nailed directly into her sides. As Bob said, "You need a Farmer Brown philosophy. He needed to get some seaweed or perhaps some romancing, so he built himself a boat."

The economical construction of these boats required only a few hand tools: a ripsaw to cut the side planks to shape, a cross-cut saw to cut the planks to length, a common claw hammer, a smoothing plane, and a hand drill.

In 1948 Bob brought home an 11-foot skiff that Fred Tripp had built in 1942, his last single-plank skiff. Bob used her for ten years until she was "borrowed." Twenty years later, he heard that there was a wrecked skiff on the shore. It sounded familiar, so Bob took a look. Yes, she was his old skiff and had lasted long enough for him to take her home and take off her lines. When finished, he set about building a new skiff exactly like the original.

Bob explained that the hanging knees under the decks are not for support. The deck is so short it will stand by itself. The knees, acting on the deck and in conjunction with the stem, are what keet the

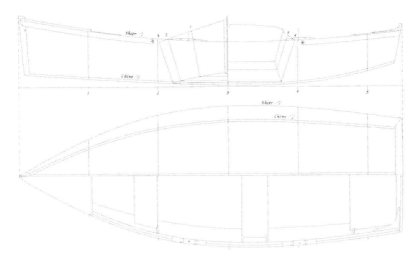

Westport Skiff
LOA: 11′0″; Beam: 3′11½″
Measured and drawn by RHB

whole from wracking. Without that stiffening, the boat would require thwart knees. "It's something to do with the whole side plank being under tension aft of the stem. The boys were backyard engineers without, I think, ever realizing it," he said.

Bob's insatiable interest was so avid that one day he grabbed me and said, "Come on, we are going to 'borrow' an old skiff from a shed about to collapse." The shed, he explained, was high on a hill overlooking the Westport River, and there was no way to get there except by boat. The boat inside, Bob knew, hadn't seen the light of day for years, and he was afraid that she would sink as soon as she was put in the water, so we grabbed a large sheet of black plastic for wrapping around her bottom and up her topsides, along with some rope and oars. Placing the gear into our own skiff, we lifted all into our truck.

After launching our own skiff in a nearby marsh, we rowed over to a beach and found the path that led up a steep hill to the shed. All I could think was how to get her down the hill without us falling down or the skiff falling apart on top of us. Actually, except for rusty fastenings, she was in quite good condition, so we gently urged her down the path of stones and dirt. Safely reaching the bottom we tightly wrapped the plastic around her bottom and up her topsides, tied her bow to our stern, and with her in tow, off we went. It wasn't long before water began to seep in, and she slowly began to sink. Rowing ever faster, we reached the marsh before she went under, bailed her out, loaded both skiffs in the truck, and disappeared before anybody saw us.

Bob named her *Southard's Skiff* after the owner, then photographed and measured her, took off her lines, researched her history, and finally called the owner and explained what we had done. The owner didn't care about the boat or even miss her, but instead of giving her to us, came and picked it up, took it home, and burned it.

Our 11-foot flat-bottomed friend, tucked up in the stern just enough to carry its load, had had its last adventure, but now, with a set of lines, she could be built again—over and over.

"There is nothing much that's new," Bob once said. "It's really old stuff reworked or modern ideas that don't work. Eventually people will return to what does work, like traditional small craft."

Southard's Skiff
LOA: 10′3½″; Beam: 3′10½″
Measured and drawn by RHB

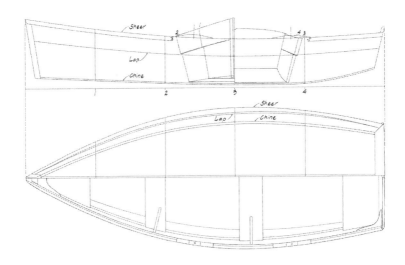

Skiffs and sharpies. From the Westport Historical Society Collection.

A Thoroughbred

Bob designed many small boats but undoubtedly the biggest challenge was when *WoodenBoat* asked him to design a car-toppable sailing canoe that could hold two people—not trolls, but real people.

Bob put a tremendous amount of thought into *Piccolo's* design, not only to make her truly seaworthy for paddling or sailing, but also to make sure she was sturdy enough to survive if she banged into a rock. Her rig had to be what one person could handle but still large enough to drive the boat. He wanted her to really sail, not just look like she might, so he decided on a ketch rig, with masts short enough to be stowed inside the boat when paddling.

Bob, never having designed or built a hull of this nature, definitely expected a few surprises - between lofting to launching. For years Bob had built tiny models, but when *Piccolo* came out of the shop and into the sunshine as a real boat, it was magical. She looked like a model, she was so dainty and delicate; a tiny and pristine gem.

Named after a small flute, *Piccolo's* details were as exquisite as those found on Goddard furniture.

The thought of Bob stepping into her seemed out of the question. But step in he did, and off he sailed, with *Piccolo* enjoying herself and doing exactly what Bob had designed her to do.

For the design and building of a tiny sailing canoe, Bob had combined his experience, observations, science, theory, and principles. Fortunately for anyone who wants to build a sailing canoe that weighs only 51 pounds and holds two people, Bob wrote two articles in *WoodenBoat* magazine, issues No. 36 and No. 37, with step-by-step instructions on how to build *Piccolo*.

Piccolo's plans, # 400-020, are available from the *WoodenBoat* Store. Her permanent home is at *WoodenBoat*'s headquarters in Brooklin, Maine.

Photographs: Personal collection.

A Swampscott Dory

Bob first found the boat, known as a North Shore Swampscott dory, while camping in the 1970s on the Belgrade Lakes, in Maine. She was lying in a pine grove, so rotten she was useless as a boat, but now, as a rare and valuable specimen of a North Shore dory, she was very important.

After Bob found owner Ben Caswell, he tried to persuade him that her condition was beyond repair, but Ben was hesitant about letting her go. His father had purchased the boat for him in 1904, and for Ben, it held years of memories. Bob visited Ben two more times (an eight-hour round trip) and finally convinced him of the importance of the dory and the need to get a set of her lines before she became mulch.

Finally Ben said, "Okay."

The Swampscott dory, named *Tim*, had been built by E. Gerry Emmons around 1900. Emmons had several shops and was well

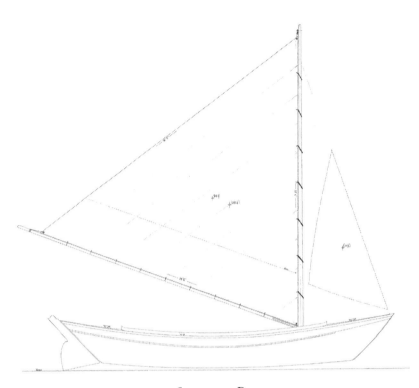

Swampscott Dory
LOA: 17' ¾"; Beam: 4'8 ¼"
Measured and drawn by RHB

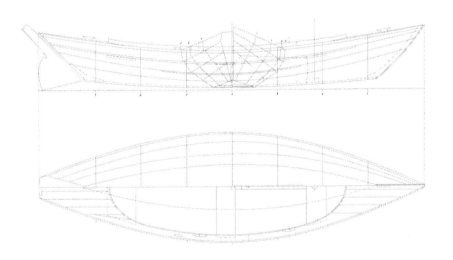

known for his fine, double-ended Swampscott-style gunning dories used for duck hunting around Marblehead, Massachusetts. He was one of the first builders to deck a sailing dory.

When Bob got this dory into his shop, he was facing an almost impossible job. There was little of her shape left, but he was determined to get a set of lines, so he set her on a pair of sawhorses and started to "paste" her back together.

The stem was gone, but by using long battens, Bob was able to fair her out and take off her lines and construction details. Bob was pleased with the lines and felt she was a fine example of a well-proportioned and handsome small dory, historically a very important boat.

Photographs: Ben Caswell (dory under sail) and personal collection.

A Last Summer

By the end of 1982 Bob often complained about his lack of energy. "It's probably lead poisoning from years of scrapping paint off boats," he said, but finally agreed to see a doctor. After a series of tests, we met again with the doctor, who bluntly told us that Bob had a brain tumor. Surgery was the only choice, so an operation was scheduled. Four hours later, the surgeon appeared in the waiting room. In a gentle tone he explained that the tumor had spread and he had been unable to remove all the cancer. Then he gave me the shocking news that Bob might only live through the summer. Having an optimistic nature I felt sure he was wrong. Impossible. I can cure him, I decided. But after a few weeks he was not improving, so I changed his diet to macrobiotic—a diet that promises to combat cancer. By mid-summer it became obvious that the diet was not helping either. Of all the challenges we had survived, this was the biggest, and beyond anything we could have imagined. It seemed impossible. Bob had promised me he would live to be ninety.

Devastated as we both were, it was a time not be wasted, so I suggested we use a tape recorder to archive his life's work. Bob, instead of growling, agreed. He knew that what he had learned, collected, and produced was important, and I knew that only he could describe his boat plans, files, photos, research, letters, etc.—and their background. Bob's way of filing was thirteenth-century: pre-typewriters, computers, or labels. It was helter-skelter. If something was filed at all, it was in a way that only he understood. Knowing that I would be responsible after he died, I had to learn what was what and where. His life's work was too important to ignore at this stage. I suggested tape-recording his thoughts while we looked through his collection.

I started with the plans drawers, all six of them filled to the top, and all six of them arbitrarily arranged. Starting with the top one by pulling out a plan, showing it to Bob, and with the recorder running, I'd ask him questions such as what was he thinking when he designed the boat or when taking lines off another? What had been his inspiration and what did he feel or learn about existing boats? Sometimes he'd answer nicely and sometimes he was sassy. And when there was a boat with only one sheet, I'd ask if there were other sheets that belonged with the one we were looking at. "Yep," he'd say, "I think there are two more sheets somewhere." So I gave the plan a number, noting that more sheets were probably in other drawers. With Bob's guidance, I was able to find all the odd sheets and put them where they belonged, like orphans who had been reunited with their families.

Bob's collection of letters he wrote or received concerning a particular boat, his photograph collection, day books, journals, and general research notes were in no better order that his plans, so we attacked them, too.

By the end of the summer, Bob had difficulty talking and staying awake.

On September 18, 1983, surrounded by his friends, Bob quietly succumbed to the cancer. He was fifty-six years old.

Photograph: personal collection.

The Two-Forty

On the day of Bob's funeral, Lance Lee, who had arrived from Maine, asked if he could take a look at Bob's plans. In a short time he pulled out a plan of a 20-foot gaff-rigged sloop that Bob had designed in 1949 at the age of twenty-two. Bob had named the design the Two-Forty of Westport. I watched as Lance studied it for a minute, and then his tongue slowly crept out—a sure sign he had found inspiration.

"This is a message in artistry to give to the apprentices and the world," Lance said. "It has the fineness of lines and proportions that have always distinguished Baker boats—a perfect marriage between function and aesthetics." Lance knew he would build the Two-Forty at the Apprentice Shop in Rockland, Maine.

In the summer of 1984, the Two-Forty was launched. Not only was she beautiful, but her trials proved her to be light, free, and incredibly responsive. By August of 1985, her trials over, she was ready to make her debut at the Newport WoodenBoat Show, with the name *Robert H. Baker* painted on her transom. But not before a second launching took place at Westport Point, Massachusetts, the waterfront village where Bob grew up and not far from where the Two-Forty had been designed.

The day was warm with a southerly breeze—just enough to make the water sparkle. More than 300 people gathered on the wharf at Westport Point, patiently waiting for the *Robert H. Baker* to roll off its trailer and into the water. Once launched and her sails raised, the *Robert H. Baker* sailed back and forth. Everyone who watched that lovely boat tacking, jibing, running, and reaching fell in love with her.

The boat, freed from paper, had come alive. The vision belongs to Lance; the design belongs to Bob; the construction belongs to the apprentices who accepted the challenge to create a functional art form.

Two-Forty
LOA: 20′2″; Beam: 7′6″

Lance Lee commented, "The *Robert H. Baker* is more than a boat. It is a marriage of function and aesthetics, nature and the nature of things, the only system of life that works in our environment. When we don't understand this system, we flounder in an alien place and it becomes an environmental miscarriage. Bob was in touch with this system, and his message for us comes through this boat."

God bless you Bob Baker. God bless you Lance Lee. God bless the apprentices.

Bob always said the only reason for being in a boat was to stay out of the water, so please, God, don't let her sink.

The *Robert H. Baker* was later sold to a family from Long Island, New York.

Photograph: Rockland Apprenticeshop.

Grand Old Ladies Don't Die Easily

For years after we sold *Kalmia* in 1968, I didn't know where she might be or if she still existed, and when near a boatyard I never dared to look, fearing I would see her rusted smokestack sticking out of the mud.

But, it seems, grand old ladies don't die easily.

One day, a Friday in 1992, nine years after Bob had died, I answered the phone and heard a woman introduce herself as Jane Ruark. She said that she and her husband owned the Deagle Boatyard in Virginia, and that she was calling concerning a particular boat. This wasn't unusual, since I've been in touch with many "boat people" since Bob passed away. Usually the inquiry was about some boat that Bob had designed or built, or had the plans for, or knew about. I asked her what boat, but her answer wasn't clear. She pronounced it again. It sounded like *Katama*, the name of a fiberglass sloop Bob had designed in 1969. To be sure I asked her to spell it.

K-A-L-M-I-A.

"*Kalmia?*" I whispered. Speechless, my eyes overflowing, I fell into my chair, deeply shocked to realize how much *Kalmia* had been a part of who Bob was.

"*Kalmia?*" I repeated. A big, long, old boat with a blue stack?

"Yes," she said.

"Oh my God," I said, "After all these years."

Clearing my throat, I listened as she explained that the boat had been left at their yard by a young couple about three years ago. Unable to follow their dreams, they had abandoned her and were nowhere to be found. *Kalmia* had been trying her best to stay afloat, but now after three years, her hull was leaking badly and her decks rotting.

"We love the boat, and would like to restore her," Jane continued,

"but right now we are too busy." She then explained that *Kalmia*
would be going up for auction in three days and felt that whoever
bought her would probably break her up for salvage, not unlike what
had almost happened before. The only comfort I got from this news
was her kind offer to let me take from *Kalmia* any mementos I might
want.

"The newel post," I said.

"But," she said, "a small bit of hope still dangles. A man who
might be interested in restoring her would be arriving over the weekend." For the next two days I counted the hours wondering if the
man would buy her, or if I should just go and see *Kalmia* myself to
bid her a final farewell. But I didn't have the courage and decided it
was better to just remember her the way she was.

On Monday, my heart pounding and fingers crossed, I called the
boatyard. *Kalmia* had survived the auction. She had been bought by
William W. Kenney, a grand nephew of John Duff, who had owned
Kalmia in 1927. Kenney's plan was to restore her. I hung up and let
out a deep breath, one that I had been holding for three days. *Kalmia*
was saved again.

Two years later, unable to raise money for *Kalmia*'s repairs, Kenney decided to sell her. He was delighted when two lawyer types

came to look at the boat. Their sleek wrinkle-free city clothes and brown leather briefcases suggested business. They explained that they had come from a marine museum in Florida. After looking *Kalmia* over, they told Kenney that if he could deliver *Kalmia* to the Miami Museum they would be happy to take her. Relieved that *Kalmia* would be taken care of, Kenney agreed.

But yesterday's history too often conflicts with today's hustlers.

Three-quarters of the way down the Intracoastal Waterway, Kenney received a message: "Due to a lack of funding, the museum no longer can take the boat." Far from home and with *Kalmia* leaking badly, Kenny decided to turn into the nearest boatyard, not realizing that the average yard would know little about hauling out an eighty-seven-year-old boat that was 83 feet long and 14 feet wide. The boatyard where he arrived proceeded to lift her out of the water with only a single strap around her middle. She broke in half and the following day was vandalized.

Fortunately, very old boats like *Kalmia* and especially if Lawley-built, are of great historic interest. When Marge Pratt, curator of the Maritime and Yachting Museum, in Stuart, Florida, heard what had happened to *Kalmia*, she immediately rushed to the boatyard to save what artifacts she could for display in her museum. A year later the Lawley Boat Owners Association held a memorial service for *Kalmia* at the USS Constitution Museum in Boston.

Kalmia is gone, but not the people who remembered her.

Photographs: Personal collection.

Epilogue

This book covers only a part of Bob's life work. In addition, there were tugs, steam packets, oyster boats, scow schooners, duck boats, crab boats, bugeyes, cats, dories, smacks, sloops, feluccas, ferries—and notebooks filled with lines he'd taken but hadn't had time to draw on paper. Bob was especially looking forward to a grant from the National Endowment for the Arts, that would give him an opportunity to document the sailing workboats of this country.

Without Bob's vision, without the hours spent in boatyards—New York, Connecticut, Rhode Island, Massachusetts, Maine, California, and in between—searching for our maritime past, how little would we know about the history of small craft, about boats married to the sea and the sky? Every deserving boat he discovered was surveyed visually, photographed, measured, and often, brought home to join others in the backyard.

After Bob died, I tried to keep the boat shop open with the help of Julia Ferguson, who had been working recently with Bob. But the shop was something much deeper than a boat on its molds and the smell of cedar. It was Bob. Why was this? I think he answered this himself when he wrote: "All things are, because they developed from a need. The need creates the mold, a parent. To preserve this mold is all-important. The preservation of a life style follows. We only look back in order to go ahead when we understand the birth of the idea."

He was a man more interested in the journey than the goals.

.... *Just ease her when she pitches* ....

Appendix I
For the Love of Boats

Two years after Bob died I was on the top floor of our leaking barn cleaning out junk when I unearthed an album. I was stunned when I opened it and discovered 114 pages of Bob's designs and sketches dating from 1943 to 1953, when Bob was sixteen to twenty years old. Why it was in the barn and perilously close to a leaking roof I'll never know.

Some designs were in ink, but most were drawn with a pencil—with lines as fine as a spider's thread. Fortunately, many included a scale and could be built. However, the paper Bob had used was dimestore stuff and had aged badly, but the drawings were still legible despite darkened and stained areas.

Following are some samples:

Swampscott Dory, 11'2"

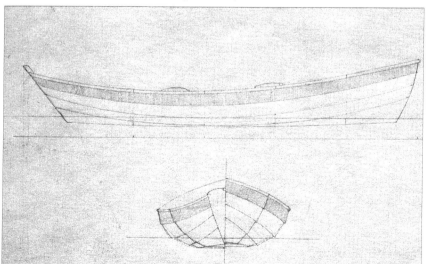

Schooner Mystery, 52′9″

Cutter, 33′9″

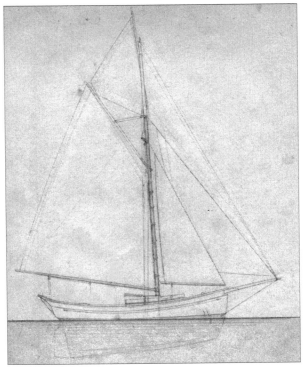

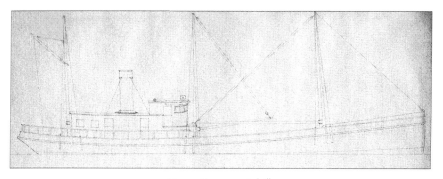

Oyster Steamer, 60′0″

Paddle Steamer, 60′0″

Diesel Tug, 39′

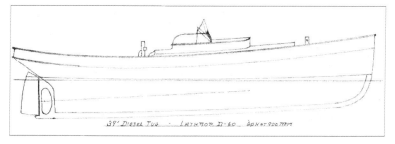

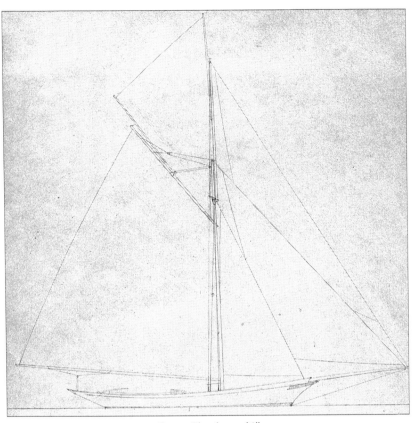

Cutter Phoebe, 47′6″

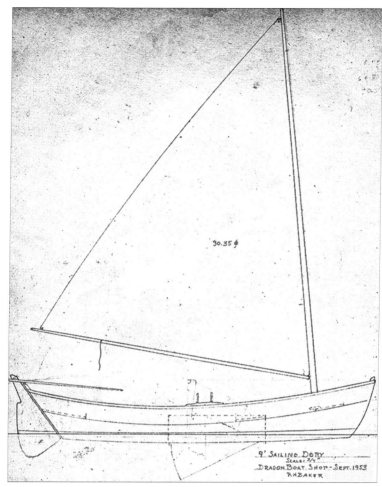

30.35 ∮

9' SAILING DORY
SCALE: 3/4
DRAGON BOAT SHOP - SEPT. 1953
R.H.BAKER

Sailing Dory, 9′0″

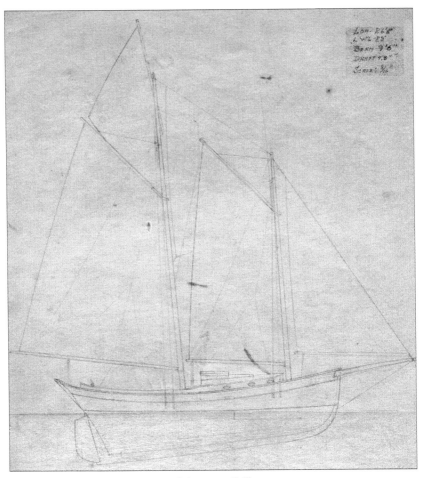

Schooner, 26'6"

Cutter, 27′0″

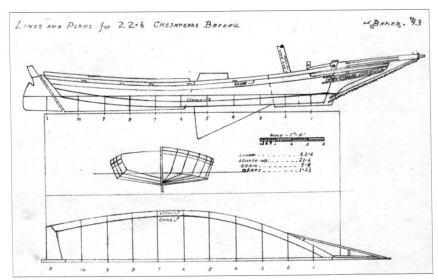

Chesapeake Bateau, 22′0″

Sharpie Nancy R, *15′0″*

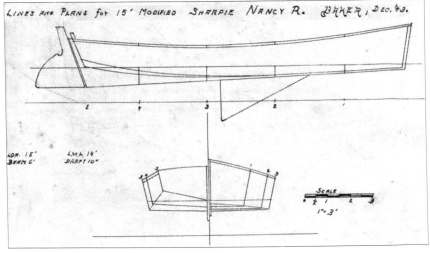

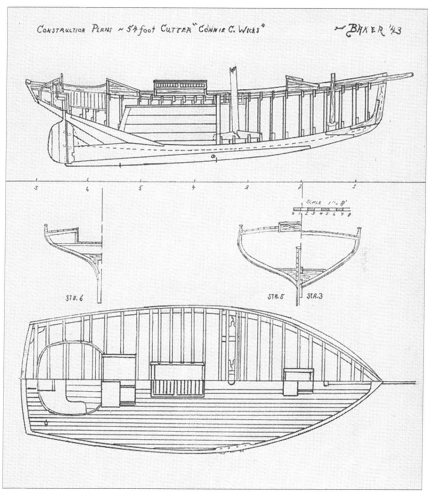

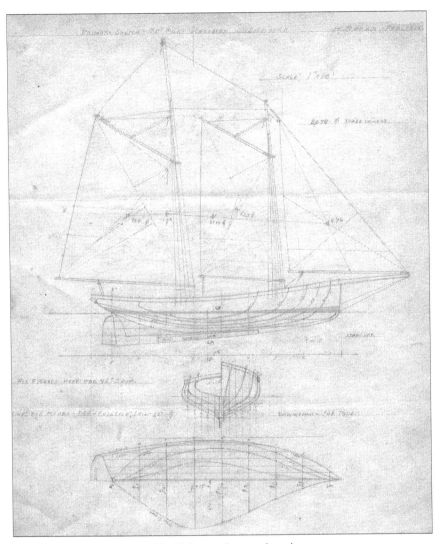

Pilot Schooner Susannah, 45′

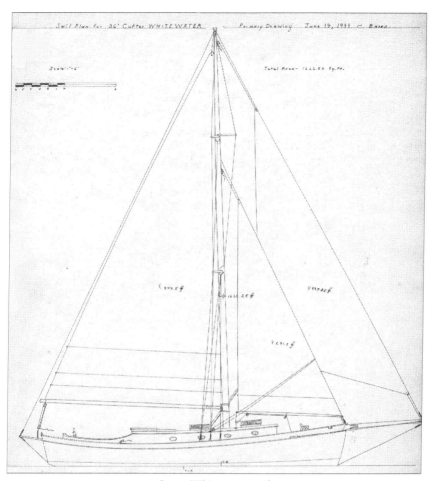

Cutter Whitewater, *36′*

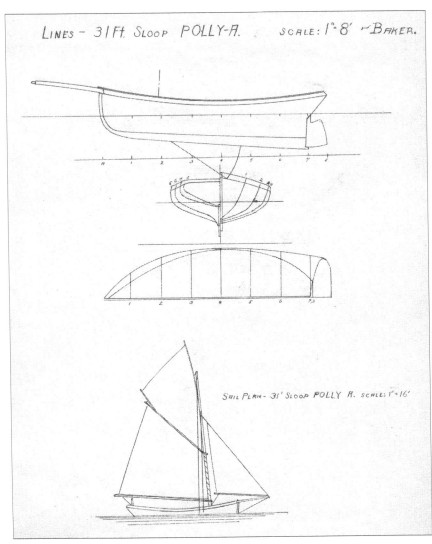

Sloop Polly A, *31'*

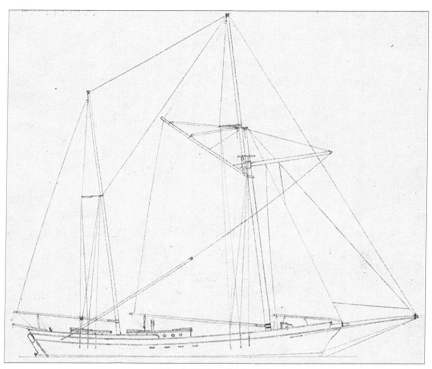

Ketch Flying Fish, *86'*

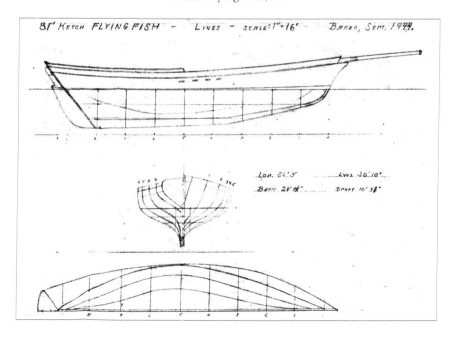

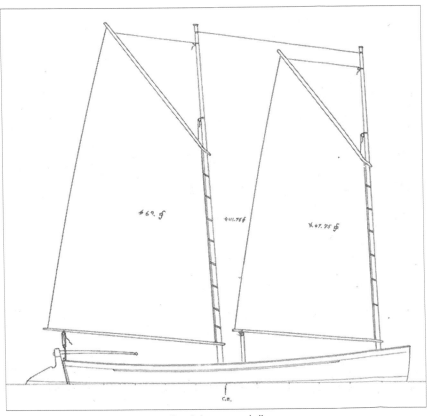

Cat Schooner, 15′0″

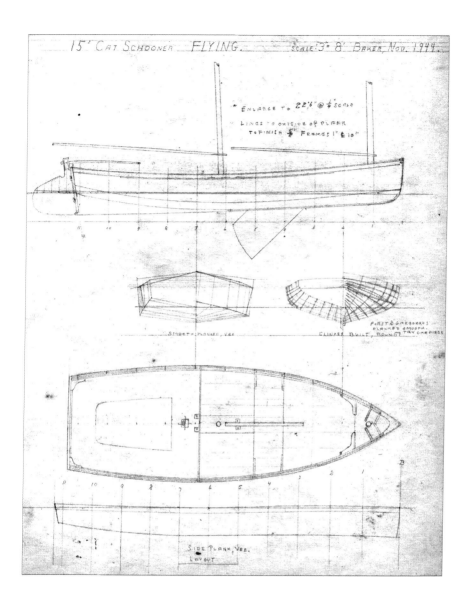

15' CAT SCHOONER FLYING. SCALE 3"=8' BAKER, Nov. 1944.

ENLARGE TO 22'6" @ ½ SCALE

LINES TO OUTSIDE OF PLANK
TO FINISH ⅝ FRAMES 1" x 10"

SMOOTH PLANKED, VEE.

FIRST 2 GARBOARDS
PLANKED SMOOTH
TRY ONE PIECE

CLINKER BUILT, ROUND.

SIDE PLANK, VEE.
LAYOUT

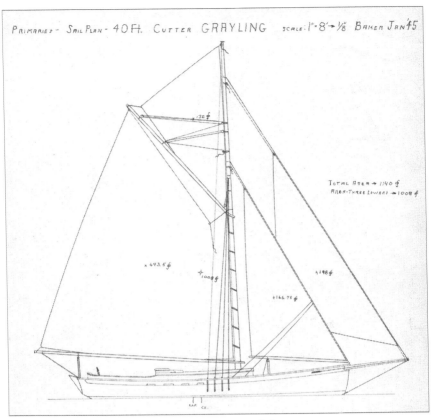

Cutter Grayling, *40′0″*

Ketch Ariel, *24′0″*

Dinghy Evening Star, *10′0″*

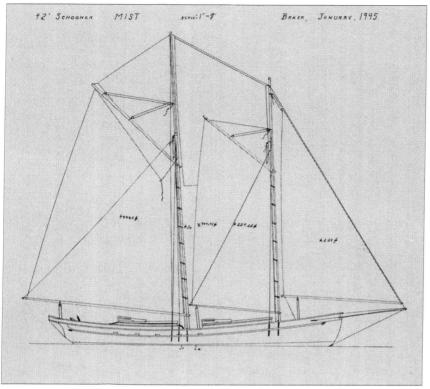

Schooner Mist, *42'0"*

Some Sketches

THE MISSING DORY
—II—
GRAND BANKS

BARQUE
LIGHTNING

SMALL GLOUCESTERMAN

GREYHOUND of the SOUND
STEAMER FAIRMONT, ICELINES

PATENS of BOSTON TUGS

NIGHTING SAILOR

WATCH of the CUTTER
FLEET of BOSTON

WESTWAY HARBOUR ENTRANCE
from
GIFFORD'S ROCK

SLOOP MISTY
of NEWPORT

WATCH WHITE WATER
of
NARRAGANSETT PIER

SOUND STEAMER
NEW LONDON

10 GUN BRIG BOXER
UNITED STATES NAVY

FISHERMAN
RIDING
BANKS

NEW YORK '90
IN HEAVY WEATHER

CATBOAT YONKER

BERMUDA MORA JIB
of
WEST PORT

ENGLISH RACING CUTTER

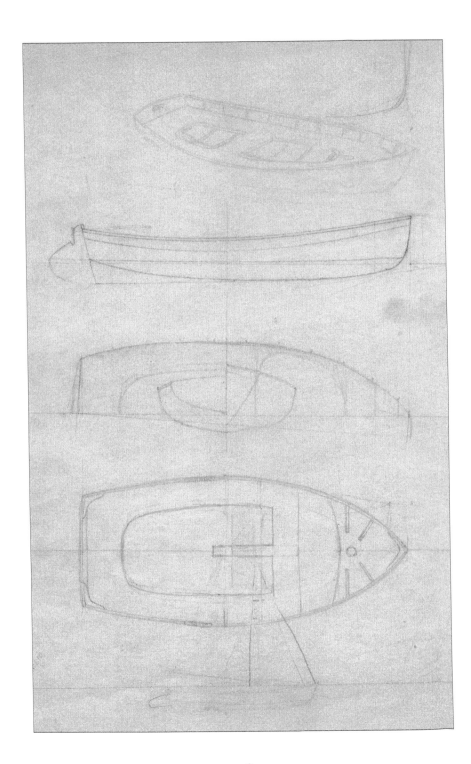

Bottoms Up my Dandy Salvage Tug
Scale 1/8"

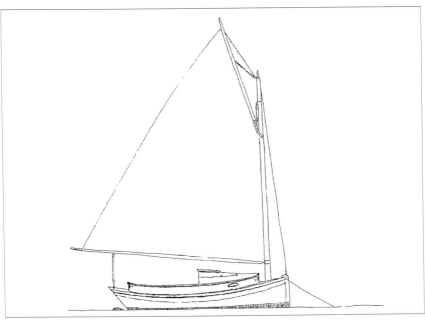

Appendix II
High School Senior Thesis, 1945

Bob attended high school at Rindge Technical School, Cambridge, Massachusetts, and graduated June 1945 at the age of seventeen. Following is what remains of the "final draft" of his senior thesis. The wording has not been changed except to add footnotes and correct minor grammatical errors.

The Principles of Marine Architecture: One of the Oldest Sciences
    By Robert H. Baker
    Homeroom 335
    January 1945

    I. The hull
        A. Resistance
            i. Surface Resistance
            ii. Eddy Resistance
            iii. Wave Resistance
        B. Curve of Area
            Shape and Discussion of
        C. Seaworthiness
            General Discussion
   II. Sails
        A. Type of Rig
        B. Position of Centers
  III. Cabin Arrangement
        General Discussion
  IV. Construction
        A. Strength of
        B. Drying Effect
        C. Result of Aging and Working
  V. Conclusion

References:
Common Sense of Yacht Design – L. F. Herreshoff
Elements of Yacht Design – Norman Skene
Yacht Designing and Planning – H. I. Chapelle

Ch. I - The Hull
I. Introduction

In this paper it is my design to discuss the practical end of yacht design without going into the theories and calculations too extensively. As long ago as early Egyptian times there have been yachts for the Pharaohs and high officials. From this long line of yachts, we have in the modern times an exact science of yacht design. I mean to discuss here the designing of a modern yacht and the various things that must be taken into consideration.

One of the best ways to study yacht design is to watch a ship under way. If we watch a sailing ship under sail, we see that there are three principal resistances to be considered. First, surface resistance, then eddy making, and last, wave resistance.

I-A: Resistance
i. Surface Resistance

With hulls traveling at low speed, surface resistance makes up nearly all the resistance. You might be apt to think that a semi-spherical hull like the one used by the "wise men of Gotham"[1] would move through the water easiest because it has the least surface area of any shape. Water, with its capillary attraction, adheres to moving shapes so that each following foot of surface has less resistance, for a film of moving water runs along with it. If you have ever compared the wake of, say, a catboat with that of a racing sloop, you will see that the cat leaves a very confused wake, while the sloop leaves a smooth following sea. So we see that the more elongated shape has the least surface resistance.

The amount of area below the waterline has much to do with surface resistance. This is why the deep fin-keeler and catamaran are so slow in light airs. In the past twenty years it is probably the improvement in the underwater profile that has increased the speed of the modern yacht more than the increased driving power of the rig.

Some years ago several New York 30s came up to race with the Newport 30s. The race was held on a day when the wind was light and variable. The New York 30s won the race quite easily, because the Newport 30s were a deep-fin type and the New York 30s were of the bulb type. This proves better than anything I can say that the surface resistance of the bulb-keeler is much less than that of the fin-keeler. Therefore we see that the fin-keeler with her deep forefoot is not as good as the bulb-keeler in a race. If you can cut down surface resistance, no matter what the rig, you will have a faster model.

ii. Eddy Resistance

Eddy resistance is closely connected with surface resistance. Variation in the underbody other than that of surface area is what we must consider now. If we are in a deep, narrow cutter close-hauled on the wind, we see that the water to windward is moved most. If we are in a shoal-draft boat, such as the centerboarder, the water to leeward is moved most. In either case this unsymmetrical displacement causes a sidelong rush of water across the forefoot, along the keel, and even aft to the rudder. In some cases, a sharp forefoot literally tears through the water at the angle of heel. Besides this, the sail is pushing the hull off to leeward.

If you watch the wake of a large sailer, you will see large eddies coming from deep down even as far as a mile astern. The creation of these eddies must represent a large amount of wasted energy. To rectify this we must attempt to keep the centerlines of any heeled hull working in unison. The cigar shape on a bulb keel might seem to be the way out, but this is bad because the hull is moving through water that is moving to leeward on the surface. We know that surface water moves to leeward in a breeze. Also the water farther down is moving to leeward at a decreasing rate the further down you go.

The wake of a deep sailer often sags off to leeward several degrees when viewed from dead astern. This is because the surface water is moving to leeward faster than the lower water where the keel is. Therefore there is good reason for the modern hull with the wide deck line aft. This is because the leeward quarter of the heeled hull carries the lines off to leeward when a properly proportioned the hull and keel are working in unison. In the yacht that has the same centerlines when heeled as when standing, the hull near the surface tries to go to leeward with the surface water while the keel tries to hold a more weatherly course. This, of course, makes bad eddies.

On a ship that carries a heavy weather helm, the rudder sets up bad eddies. One way to correct this is to have the center line of the yacht become curved as she heels. We all know that when a wide centerboarder heels, the waterline to leeward becomes more curved and straightens out to windward as her weather side rises out of the water. This causes the boat to head into the wind. In a deep, narrow boat, the curve to windward is greater than the leeward side. Therefore she tends to head off the wind and must be stopped by her rudder. The narrow hull is best to use with a high rig that throws its driving power well to leeward when heeled, for the lateral plane moves aft. On a vessel with a straight keel and deep forefoot, there is a marked tendency to yaw in a following sea. This of course sets up eddies under the forefoot. To stop this, a slight forefoot with a nicely rockered keel should be employed.

iii. Wave Resistance

A vessel moving through the water must push out of her way a volume of water equal to her displacement. This movement is in the form of waves, both bow waves and following waves. In moderation, it would seem logical to use a sharp entrance and clean run. This is all very well, but a run that is too fine will allow the first following wave to build up under the center and provide a bad drag. All this is closely tied in with the curve of areas. Too many modern designers take the foregoing resistance too much to heart and draw the 'ideal' curve of area before they draw the lines. I find it better, and not a little easier, to draw the lines first. Drawing a shape that looks well, is easy to construct and taking into consideration the resistances.

I-B: Curve of Area

The curve of areas must follow some definite plan, however. It is well to try to locate the center, or greatest area, somewhere near the center of lateral plane. The centers should come about 50 to 60% of the waterline length aft. This is good for steering in a following sea and also put the center of buoyancy close to the center of oscillation. The closer you can bring these two, the less power will be lost through pitching.

I-C: Seaworthiness

Seaworthiness is of even greater importance then speed in the cruiser. It depends on many things, among which is whether you want a good boat for high or low speed. A boat that is dry at low speed is usually extremely wet at high speeds. Some say that our American Whalers were about the best sea boats for their speed. But if you speeded one of them up, the affect would be terrible. The long lean bows on the later Gloucestermen were very good for slow to moderate speeds, while the full bows on Captain Slocum's sloop *Spray* were both wet and uncomfortable.

If every country in the word were asked what they considered most important in a sea boat, the chances are that everyone would want a good sheer and a double-ended hull. The good sheer is one of the most important with respect to shipping solid water. It is remarkable how low the freeboard amidships can be and still not ship water if the bow and stern are high. A high stern is most appreciated after you have been pooped by a following sea a few times. It is amazing how low the free board can be amidships without shipping water if the ends are high.

The double-ender is about the best shape for out-tosea work. With her sharp bow she will cut the waves forward, taking the head seas, and her sharp stern will do the same aft over a following sea. If we were to use a design with a wide flat stern, we would see the buoyancy of it would force the bows into every big sea. Thus if you must have a transom, keep it narrow and sharp for sea work. Or, if you must have a wide stern, keep a wide deck line forward to counteract it. Some bright onlookers will probably ask about this point, "How are you going to incorporate all this in one boat?" Well, I have tried to illustrate that in the accompanying drawings. [Unfortunately the original Thesis that was turned in is lost, and so, too, are the drawings.]

The sections of a boat have something to do with the amount a boat will roll in a beam sea. The wine glass section with its slack bilges will roll most of all and no amount of sail will steady her. In some cases this is good because it will keep her from ducking her rails every time she rolls. But it makes a very uncomfortable boat if you are trying to get some sleep or catch a hot meal. Like the Block Islanders say, "A rolling boat is a good sea boat, but hell to live aboard." Just the opposite of this is the flat floor and hard bilge of a steamer. The hard bilge tends to deaden the roll, but it makes a wet boat. Therefore the cruiser should have a section that has the hard bilges of one and the great deadrise of the other.

Ballast must also be taken into consideration briefly as it has much to do with the rolling of the boat. A boat with all her ballast outside tends to roll worse than a hull having ballast inside spaced well out in the frames athwartships. If ballast is all bunched together in the 'midship section, the boat will pitch badly in a head sea. There is no doubt that raising the center of weight is one way to get easy motion, but the lower the weight the greater the ability to carry sail in a gale. Therefore space the ballast both fore and aft and athwartships.

While on the subject of hull shapes, docking and hauling must be considered. Boats with great drag to the whole keel are difficult to dock and make it necessary to use a great deal of blocking while hauling. But if the drag is put into the forward part of the keel and the after part, say 75 percent of the whole keel, is straight, this difficulty is overcome.

When designing the cruiser, it is best to keep clear of all race rules. The modern racing rules have produced a boat that is neither fast nor seaworthy. This is shown by comparison of *Tioga*, a modern cruiser by L. Francis Herreshoff and *Istalena*, a modern racer also designed by him. *Tioga* was a little shorter and had much less sail while her displacement was much greater. *Tioga* averaged ten knots between New London and Marblehead, which he says the racer never could have equaled. *Tioga* was a much easier boat and had cruising accommodations as well.

When designing a new hull, it is well to keep in mind the preceding facts and also: ease of construction, cabin accommodations, fairness, and cost as well as the balance of centers.

Ch. II Sails

II. Introduction

In discussing sails, I think it would be better to forget about the aerodynamics of sails and look to the more practical side of rigs. Until about ten years ago the rig was designed by a person to meet the requirements of a particular locality. In recent years, however, the designer has taken to moderating the more common types so they are good in all localities. This may or may not be good, depending on your own opinion. It still stands, however, that certain types are used for certain purposes.

II-A. Type of Sails

The cat, for instance, has been the universal type for a small daysailer between Cape Cod and Newport. Also it has found great popularity in and around Barnegat Bay. The cat rig has quite a few drawbacks that are very apparent in the poorly designed boat. The hull, for one thing, is rather short and beamy. This can produce a very slow and heavy boat if improperly designed. The large single sail is one of its good points. It has the most driving power for its area because there is no danger of the jib backwinding it. The main trouble with the cat is perhaps steering, as the speed of the boat increases there is a marked increase in weather helm. Therefore it is wise to place the center of effort well ahead of the center of lateral resistance. This will in part eliminate the weather helm. And because the mast is usually unstayed, the old Cape men used to say you could carry sail longer. That is because when a squall hits, the mast will bent and spill the wind. With the cat, a Marconi or Leg o' Mutton sail shouldn't be used. When these are used, there is too much change of the center when reefed down. In small cats the spritsail should be used instead of the usual gaff.

In recent years the sloop has found favor both with cruisemen and racers. The advantage of the sloop is that the large area of the cat has been broken down into two sails. Each sail has a tendency to revolve around its axis, so the center of effort doesn't move aft so much. With proper handling, the two sails can be set so that the boat will sail herself. This is particularly useful in single-handed cruising because you can do some work about the deck or catch a meal without heaving-to. Another advantage is that the mast is far enough aft so that stays can be employed. Thus a lighter spar can be used. It is customary to break up the forward triangle on the larger sloops into two or more headsails. In the last few years it has become the practice to make the rig very tall and narrow under the impression that the upper two-thirds of the sail does the most work. This may be true in theory, but I don't think that you could cut off the lower third and get the same per-formance and speed. It is bad practice in all but the most highly developed racers as the tall rig puts that much more weight up aloft which in turn causes the boat to roll badly in a sea. Also the high rig with its extra tall spar makes the weight aloft too great for good cruising. When something happens aloft the top of the mast sways so much more than a short one that it is difficult if not impossible to work. When designing a hull for a sloop rig, re-member the center of effort will come fairly far aft, so the keel will need a fair amount of drag, or a centerboard quite far aft.

Until ten years or so ago the schooner rig was considered the best for both work boats and ocean cruisers. The schooner is a highly developed rig that takes some practice to design properly. The main drawback is that it requires a fairly large crew to work her efficiently. The schooner rig, if properly proportioned, can be sailed under several combinations of sails. In heavy winds, she can be hove-to under either foresail or triple reefed mainsail. Large schooners have usually two or more headsails and a gaff topsail on both or just the main. When designing the hull, you should keep in mind that the center of effort is low in comparison with the length, so the hull can be lighter and finer than the average. The center of effect will come somewhere near the leach of the foresail, so the keel can be nearly straight. If a centerboard is used, it should be right forward of the main mast. The schooner rig in small boats is not practical because the sail is chopped up into pieces that are too small. However, there have been boats built up around Tancook Island, Nova Scotia, which have been very good. The modern staysail and wishbone rigs are a good thing to stay clear of. The heavy wishbone rig on the forestaysail is too heavy for comfortable handling.

The ketch is the oldest rig still in use. It was used years ago as the famous "Bomb Ketch" of the British and French navies. In late years it has become popular as a cruising boat. It has for some time been popular on Chesapeake Bay in the form of the cat ketch. It has few advantages not found in the sloop or yawl and has some serious disadvantages, such as when the sail area becomes large, it becomes very hard to handle. But as there have been few large cruisers built in recent years, this is not serious. The ketch is the only rig that can be reefed down without changing the center of effort. She can be sailed under any sensible combination of sail and the large mizzen is a good sail under which to heave-to. This is one of the objections of the yawl. The real objection is that the mizzen will probably come right where you wanted to locate the engine. This is overcome by mounting the engine and wheel off center.

The yawl rig is similar to the ketch rig and when the mizzen is large, the same particulars hold true of either rig. The yawl with a small mizzen is practically a sloop. They are about as fast and should be rated with them, for the mizzen is too small for laying-to.

The cat ketch or cat yawl were once popular along our Atlantic coast. This rig is a practical one, because it embodies the principles of both the cat and the ketch or yawl. It has, however the disadvantage of the cat, that of being hard to stay the mainmast. At this point we could go into the aerodynamics of sails, but I think enough has been said about sails to point out the various points of the various rigs.

Square sails are finding popularity with many American offshore cruising men. They say that when running before the wind they are as efficient as the rest of the sail put together. However, when running before a high sea, the backwind from the sea in front of you is likely to backwind the sail and cause considerable damage both aloft and to the hull if he broaches to. In Mr. Robinson's attempt to revive the early American sailing craft he has made extensive use of square sail. This is all very well on a slack reach or a following wind, but on a tight bowline or a tack they are useless and demand a large crew to handle them.

Square sails have been rigged on both ketches and schooners to good effect, but on a sloop they are next to useless. There is some use to the square cat, however. When running in a moderate sea it will serve to push you along at a good speed. Many designers make the mistake of making the yard of the sail too long. On a small boat you don't want to go out on a pitching yard arm to furl the sail. It is best to make the yard short and the foot long so that the yard can be sent down to furl the sail. As foresails such as the quadrilateral jib are not used extensively, we won't discuss them.

II-B. Position of the Centers
So much for the type of rig, now we must consider the position of the centers. There have been many 'ideal' proportions for the area of sail set up, but I think the best guide is comparison with other boats of their type and tonnage. The main thing is that when you have found the center of effort, it should be somewhere near the middle of the overall length. When the center of effort and the lateral plane have been laid down, the center of effort should be located forward of the lateral plane. Failure to have this forward will make the boat carry a heavy windward helm and be hard to put about. If the center is too far forward of the lateral plane, the boat will have a tendency to fall off the wind. The lead should range anywhere from .05 to .2 of the waterline length, depending on the type of rig and which designer you ask.

Everyone has his own ideas on this. I, for one, think that if it looks reasonable, it will sail fairly well. I have had some leads that were too close, according to the experts, which sailed very well. The center of effort, lateral plane, and the center of buoyancy or the greatest surface area should be located fairly near each other. There is no set rule for this, but the closer they are the less power will be wasted in pitching and rolling.

Ch. III - Cabin Arrangement

III. Introduction

On the subject of cabin arrangement, there is not much to be said by me. This must be left to the individual designer. Some points in general can be made, however. On the subject of arrangement and position of galleys too much cannot be said.

In too many of our modern yachts, the galley has been neglected. It has been shoved off in one corner without sufficient ventilation or light. The galley is the center of the offshore cruiser. There is a pot of hot coffee on the 'Shipmate' for the watch at night and the Sunday dinner must be cooked here. The galley should be located at the after end of the house where it is handy both to the watch, and in the single-hander, the helm. The companion way also helps to ventilate and light it. Some thought should go into the size and type of stove and size of worktables. If the boat is going to sleep four people, you can't feed them all on a small two burner primus. The coal, coke, or wood range is perhaps the best for extended cruising, whereas the smaller coal-oil and alcohol primus is enough for an occasional meal or pot of coffee. If she is to be used in cold weather, the stove must be able to heat the whole cabin. As to worktables, we would have them big enough to be practical, but not in the way.

Some consideration must be given to the finish of the cabin. White paint is probably best, as it is easy to clean and keeps the cabin light and cheerful. Varnish and stain make the cabin dark and cold to the eye. In former years, white elm was used unfinished in yacht cabins because it got whiter and whiter with continued scrubbing.

Ch. IV - Construction

IV. Introduction

In discussing the construction of our yacht, we will talk in general terms and not in particular. When discussing construction there are certain things to be remembered. First, the strength of the complete structure, next the change in shape due to the drying effect of the timber drying and aging.

IV-A. Strength of Construction

The strength of the hull, contrary to popular belief, is not dependent on size of the timber, but rather on the kind of timber and the style of fasting. As to the kind of timber, it is fairly clear that you wouldn't frame up a workboat with soft pine. Common sense and a slight knowledge of the properties of the different woods is the best guide. I have been aboard various boats and heard the owner boast about what a strong boat he had and then go and point to the heavy oak cabins and frames with thick hanging knees alongside of them. In most cases the beams have pulled away from the frame heads and cabins so that you could see a good deal of light through the paint. The hanging knees had shrunk until they no longer bore on their landings or had cracked wide open. It is a wonder to me that the boats hold together at all. This trouble, as you can see, is due to improper fastening. When fastening beams to frame heads, it is the best policy to bolt or rivet them through. In order to prevent hogging at the ends due to parting of fastenings, the cabins and shelves should be bolted to the breasthook and that in turn bolted to the stem head. The after end should be bolted to the quarter knees and these to the transom or transom frame.

IV-B. Drying Effect

The drying effect of timber on the shape of the hull is marked indeed. When a dry plank gets wet, it expands across the grain much more then with the grain, as we all know. This is something that can't be helped. This is also on of t e greatest drawbacks to plywood and other laminated woods. The wood laid on grain going in the other direction will check and draw badly when it gets wet and dries. The failure is not in the glue, but in the wood. Therefore leave plywood alone except for dry places. The force exerted by this expansion is enormous. In fact, when a boat is first launched, the expansion will literally stretch the frames. This causes the frame to straighten out somewhat and causes the sheer to flatten out. When the sheer straightens, the ends naturally droop. Therefore, as we can see, the whole shape of the boat is changed. This won't damage her sailing too much, but it produces a bad looking hull. The only good way to stop change in shape is to fasten every joint thoroughly. Ironwork, such as chainplates, must be fastened directly to a frame in large hulls. Otherwise the expansion of the plank will soon tear the plank where the bolts pass through. Another way to keep the ends from hogging is to use longitudinal frames like stringers set into heavy sawn frames and bolted to stem and stern. This is probably the best construction for racers if the timbers are kept light. In the cruiser, however, the frames take up too much room in the cabin and engine compartment. The best and cheapest way to stop hogging is to use common sense in the timbers and fastenings.

IV-C. Result of Aging and Working

Panting in a wooden hull, that is, the change of the shape of the section due to the change in stress while underway, is our next point of consideration. When a boat is built, the weight is concentrated on the keel. But when she is launched, the weight is lifted from the keel and distributed around the whole underbody. Therefore, the sections will tend to straighten out. When a sailing hull is underway, the weight and driving power are pushing down on the keel and also pulling up on the windward chain plates. The force on the chain plates is often 150 percent of the total weight of the rig and the mast pushes down with as much as 75 percent of the weight. Therefore we see that there is great strain on the hull that will change her entire shape if not properly designed to overcome this defect. The way to stop panting in a large measure is through the use of thwart ship bulkheads. There have been some very successful bulkheads made of laminated wood, but they must be fastened with long screws placed close together. Laminated wood of the plywood type tends to check and draw in a damp cabin, however. The best plan, perhaps, is to lay the bulkhead with one set of sheathing running in one direction and another set in the opposite direction. These should be fairly thick and fastened together with some sort of flexible glue such as common marine glue. Here again, careful fastening and selection of timber will reduce panting to a minimum. Remember this:

Every creak or groan in a working hull represents a joint that is slipping about. These must be reduced, and whenever possible, eliminated.

Ch. V. Conclusion

In conclusion, if you use your common sense, follow the examples set by leading architects, and remember the facts stated here you can turn out a very successful boat without too much trouble. Remember that water can be the most gentle handler on earth, but that it can also wreck a boat with one heavy sea.

1. The Wise Men of Gotham are recalled in a popular English nursery rhyme. The lyrics are:
Three wise men of Gotham,
They went to sea in a bowl,
And if the bowl had been stronger,
My song had been longer.
Opie and P. Opie, *The Oxford Dictionary of Nursery Rhymes* (Oxford: Oxford University Press, 1951, 2nd ed., 1997), p. 193.

Suggested Reading and RHB Plans

Boatbuilding: A Complete Handbook Of Wooden Boat Construction.
   Author – Howard I. Chapelle

Worthy of the Sea: K. Aage Nielsen And His Legacy Of Yacht Design.
   Authors – Maynard Bray and Tom Jackson.

Building Classic Small Craft
   Author – John Gardner.

The Dory Book
   Author – John Gardner.

Boats: A Manual for Their Documentation
   Editors – Paul Lipke, Peter Spectre. Benjamin A. G. Fuller

Designs to Inspire
   Authors – Anne and Maynard Bray

Forty Wooden Boats: A Third Catalog of Building Plans
   Author – *WoodenBoat* magazine

Boatbuilding Manual, Fifth Edition
   Author – Robert M. Steward

Collecting Houses: 17th Century – 20th Century Adventure
   Author – Anne W. Baker

Articles by RHB written for *WoodenBoat* magazine:
   Issue 1, p. 20: Building the Sailing Dinghy *Nellie* (Bembo)

Issue 23, p. 39: Building the Catboat *Peggotty*
Issue 32, p. 29: Building the Westport Skiff
Issue 32, p. 32: Keep It Simple (Tools)
Issue 32, p. 29: Letter about Westport Skiff
Issue 33, p. 5: Letter about Westport Skiff
Issue 36, p. 44: How to Build *Piccolo*: Part I
Issue 37, p. 57: How to Build *Piccolo*: Part II
Issue 45, p. 108: Rabbeting Techniques for a Whitehall

Other articles in *WoodenBoat* magazine:
Issue 66, p. 48: Simplicity, Skiffs and Sharpies, by A. W. Baker and J. Gilmore
Issue 114, p. 52: Sloop: comments, photo

Articles about Baker Boat Works in *Messing About in Boats*:
Vol. 2, Issue 22, p. 12: Carrying On The Tradition, by Bob Hicks
Vol. 3, Issue 14, p. 11: If Only Bob Could Have Seen It, by Bob Hicks

Robert H. Baker plans are available from:
Mystic Seaport Collections
(860) 572-5367
collections@mysticseaport.org

As of 2013, Mystic Seaport Collections houses all available papers having belonged to Robert H. Baker, including boat plans, photographs, notes, drawings, sketches, and other related material. Additionally, Mystic Seaport Museum has in its collections several boats having belonged to and been cared for by Bob Baker.

As of 2012, Roger Williams University Library houses all available papers having belonged Anne W. Baker relating to her work with houses, mills, and other structures primarily in the southeastern New England area.

Contact the Baker estate at: RHBakerCatalog@gmail.com

Anne W. "Pete" Baker was a restoration contractor, architectural historian, and consultant. She worked with building owners, agencies, and historians in the documentation, restoration, and preservation of over 300 seventeenth- and eighteenth-century structures in southern New England. Her book *Collecting Houses* recalls how she came to love, understand, and work with these historic buildings. Her own knowledge of wood and traditional construction complemented Bob's passion for traditional watercraft. She lived in Westport, Massachusetts, until her passing in *2011*.

Made in the USA
Charleston, SC
03 December 2014